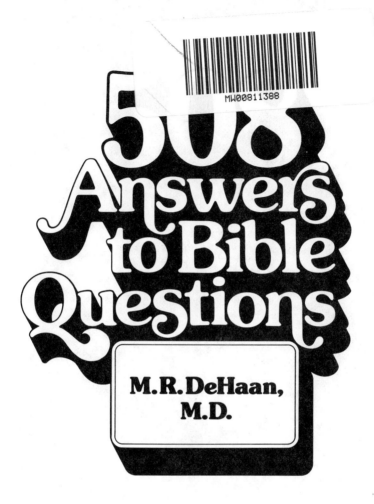

508 Answers to Bible Questions

M. R. DeHaan, M.D.

ZONDERVAN
PUBLISHING HOUSE
OF THE ZONDERVAN CORPORATION | GRAND RAPIDS, MICHIGAN 49506

508 ANSWERS TO BIBLE QUESTIONS
Copyright 1952 by
Zondervan Publishing House
Grand Rapids, Michigan

Assigned to the Radio Bible Class, 1966

ISBN 0-310-23341-0

Printed in the United States of America

83 84 85 86 87 88 — 30 29 28 27 26 25

DEDICATION

To the thousands upon thousands of our listeners who have asserted their confidence in the Radio Bible Class by sending in their problems to us for solution, and thus unknowingly providing the material for this volume, this book is gratefully dedicated.

ACKNOWLEDGMENT

To Miss Leona Hertel, my personal secretary for over eleven years, should go much, if not most of the credit for the creation of this volume. It was she who kept carbon copies of these answers as they were given in my personal correspondence over the years, in answer to the questions which came in. It was she who arranged the material in convenient and usable form for our secretaries here in the office, and who first suggested publishing the material in the form of this book.

Miss Hertel did almost all of the work of arranging, compiling and indexing this volume. With praise to God for faithful Christian secretaries, we gratefully acknowledge the valuable services rendered by this, His precious servant, without whose deep interest and help, the task of publishing this book in its present form would have been made very difficult, if not well nigh impossible.

M. R. DeHaan

INTRODUCTION

The contents of this volume consist largely of questions sent in by listeners to the RADIO BIBLE CLASS over a period of some twelve years. They represent the questions concerning Scripture problems most frequently submitted by our radio listeners. Many of the questions are asked hundreds of times by as many listeners, independently of each other. They are, therefore, questions uppermost in the minds of many, many people.

The answers to these questions represent paragraphs from personal letters written by me in answer to our listeners' inquiries. As these questions were answered by personal letter, that portion pertaining to the question was kept separate and filed in a "question and answer" book here in the office. Over the years these questions and answers grew to a large number, and are being added to constantly, as new questions not covered by previous correspondence are received.

In this volume, therefore, we have printed in this permanent form a carefully selected number of these questions and answers. The selection is on the basis of general interest to the most people, as determined by the frequency with which they have been asked by our correspondents. Many, many questions of a wholly personal, local or temporary nature have been deleted.

The compilation of these answers in an indexed form was first prepared only for use in our own offices of the RADIO BIBLE CLASS, to assist in the answering of our mail. It has been of untold value in saving a great deal of time, for both myself and the stenographers. By keeping a file of each question as it came in, it eliminated the necessity of answering the same question over and over and over again. As the questions were received, our secretaries could then turn to this file, and if the question had been previously answered they could simply use the answer in the book, thus making it unnecessary for me to answer it again. It is humanly impossible to answer the thousands and thousands of questions and problems received in the letters reaching our office each week. By keeping a record of all the answers sent out in the past, they can be used again and again, and only the new problems not covered in the "book" need to come to my attention for personal answers.

A few years ago my personal secretary suggested that this material be published in a volume available to the public. Upon her suggestion, we took the matter up with our publishers, and they immediately recommended it very enthusiastically. Now after months of compiling, proof-reading, additions, and deletions, it is ready for the public. We send it forth with a sincere prayer to our Father, in the name of His Son Jesus Christ, and trust Him to bless it unto many hearts by the precious, blessed Holy Spirit.

M. R. DeHaan

CONTENTS

CHAPTER 1

ANGELS, DEMONS AND THE DEVIL

1. Does the Bible Teach the Existence of Guardian Angels?

Yes, although the Bible does not use the expression, "guardian angels," we believe angels are sent to guard God's children. See Matthew 18:10.

> Take heed that ye despise not one of these little ones; for I say unto you, That in heaven their angels do always behold the face of my father which is in heaven.

This passage suggests strongly that God sends angels to protect little children. Whether there is an angel for each child, we do not know. (See also Hebrews 1:14)

2. Who Are the "Sons of God" in Genesis 6?

I believe the giants in Genesis 6 were the result of an unnatural union of fallen angels with the daughters of men. Notice that this was the occasion for the flood. The word in Hebrew is "nephillim" and means "the fallen ones." Incidentally, I might say that while the Bible states that angels *in Heaven* neither marry nor are given in marriage, one must remember that this is spoken of the angels *of God, in Heaven*, while these in Genesis 6 were not in heaven, but were fallen angels.

3. Were the Angels Created?

In regard to the creation of angels, we are told definitely in Psalm 148, verses 2 and 5, that they were created by the Lord. Also in Colossians 1:16 we are told, "for by Him were all things created that are in heaven, and that are in earth, visible and invisible, whether they be thrones or dominions or principalities or powers, all things were created by Him and for Him." Then again, we are told definitely that Satan, who, of course, is a fallen angel, was also a created being. In Ezekiel 28, verse 13, we are definitely told about his creation.

4. Is It Possible for Angels to Fall Today?

Concerning the possibility of angels falling today, I do not know of anything at all in the Scriptures which would indicate that angels today can fall. It seems that their fall occurred under the leadership of Satan, before the creation of the world, as recorded in Genesis 1:2. Evidently, the angels today are confirmed in their position, and therefore, cannot fall anymore.

5. I Always Understood That Michael, the Archangel, Was the Same As the Lord Jesus Christ. Is This Correct?

Michael, the archangel, is not the same as the Lord Jesus Christ. Michael, the archangel, is the particular archangel who has to do with the protection of the nation of Israel. In the few references in the Bible where Michael is mentioned, it is always with regard to the nation of Israel who will be restored to the land of Palestine and become the people of the Kingdom.

6. Can Satan Destroy Us Who Are Christians?

The Bible is absolutely clear that while Satan is powerful, he is not all-powerful. In John 10 we read that "no man shall pluck us out of the Father's hand." The word, "man," here is not in the verse in the original, so that it includes everything and everybody. The Word of God is very definite, "They shall *never* perish." We are told by John that "greater is He that is in us, than he that is in the world" (I John 4:4). You may dismiss from your mind any thought that Satan is able to pluck you out of the hand of the Saviour.

7. How Could the Devil Sin in Heaven?

In regard to your question concerning the Devil sinning in heaven, we must remember that the Devil was not a redeemed creature, and, therefore, could sin, but we who are redeemed by the blood of the Lord Jesus Christ, when we have received our resurrected bodies will be beyond all possibility of sinning. Remember that heaven, too, is going to be purified.

8. What Is Meant By "Spiritual Wickedness?"

In regard to your question concerning "spiritual wickedness," the context (Ephesians 6:12) shows that it is spiritual wickedness in high places, and undoubtedly refers to the deception of the Devil and the rulers of this present age. Today the governments of the world seem to be deceived, not knowing the grace of God.

9. Why Didn't God Destroy the Devil When He Sinned?

In answer to this question we can only point you to Deuteronomy 29, verse 29, where we read: "The secret things belong unto the Lord our God, but those things which are revealed belong unto us, and unto our children forever." God is not required to give an answer to His creatures for what He does, for since He is absolutely sovereign, He can do as He pleases. Since He has created *all* things, He is the sovereign Master of all, and these are just questions we have to leave with the Lord entirely and submit to His will. There are many, many things in the world and in our experience and in the Bible which we cannot understand, but we accept them because we believe.

10. In Studying the 28th Chapter of I Samuel, I Am Somewhat Puzzled. Was Samuel Actually Brought Back to Life Through Demon Possession by the Witch of Endor, Or Did God Permit This To Be Done?

This is a passage on which Bible students are generally greatly disagreed. There are those who claim that it was a Satanic appearance. Others claim that it was merely an illusion, while there are others who claim that God deliberately brought Samuel back, even though it was through the witch of Endor, that he might witness and testify against Saul. Certainly, it proves that the souls of our loved ones are conscious after death, and God in His sovereign purpose can bring them back if it so pleases Him. I would advise that you continue to pray about it and study it. I think that you will see that this was a sovereign act of God in warning Saul against his evil way, and permitting Samuel to come out of the grave for just that brief period of time.

11. Is Michael the Only Archangel, and If So, Who Is Gabriel?

Michael, the chief angel, is the only archangel, and has a definite and apparently exclusive commission to watch over the nation of Israel, and to protect her, and is never mentioned except in the role of protecting God's ancient covenant people, Israel.

Gabriel, the mighty angel, had a definite ministry in conveying the most important messages to man which God would not entrust to lesser beings.

12. Are There Different Orders Among the Angels?

Angels are organized in different companies and ranks for special, definite service, but individual angels have individual tasks, such as Michael and Gabriel. Some of these high-ranking angels are called "princes," denoting their high office. Satan, before his fall, himself was a high-ranking angel, probably the highest in heaven, and was called "Lucifer," the special guardian of the Throne of God, before he was lifted up with pride and cast out from the presence of Almighty God (Isaiah 14).

13. Do Angels Have Wings?

There is no verse in the Bible which presents angels as having wings. They are said to fly in a few instances, but any reference to wings of angels is quite absent. Of course, you will refer me immediately to the cherubim and the seraphim which are mentioned a few times in the Bible, especially in the book of Ezekiel, and called also "beasts" or "living creatures," as appearing over the ark of the Covenant with wings overspreading the Mercy Seat, but these are an entirely different order of beings. They are never called angels, and I do not believe that they are angels, but another order of spirit beings for a special purpose and ministry of God. They are called "beasts" or "living creatures," and have a ministry distinct and peculiar, wholly different from the angels. Angels do move swiftly, however, and we know that they can travel with the speed of light.

CHAPTER 2

BAPTISM

14. Is Water Baptism Necessary for Salvation?

We do not believe that water baptism adds one thing to our salvation. We are saved by grace and grace alone. It is the command of the Lord for us to testify to our identification in the death, burial and resurrection of Jesus Christ by being baptized. It is, as far as salvation is concerned, entirely a matter of personal light. If one believes that he should not be baptized, he would, of course, be a hypocrite if he submitted to it. However, if we believe it is for us, we would be displeasing the Lord if we did not do it. The important thing is that we can continue to love one another even though we do not agree on all points in this matter.

15. Should All Believers Be Baptized?

Yes, we believe it is the duty of every believer to submit to baptism, not as a matter of salvation, but as a matter of obedience. There is no baptism by sprinkling in the Bible. It is always (as the original Greek indicates) by immersion. Water baptism has nothing to do with our salvation, but I do believe it becomes the Christian's duty to submit to it.

16. Do You Believe that Infants Should Be Baptized?

We believe that baptism must follow conversion. Regarding children, I believe it is good to dedicate infants and children to the Lord, but dedication is not baptism. Dedi-

cation is the act of the parent, in which he presents his
child to God and assumes responsibility for the training of
that child for Him. Baptism, however, is the act of the
believer himself, in which he confesses faith in the Lord
Jesus who "died for our sins and rose again for our
justification."

17. Are All Infants and Children Saved?

The Bible nowhere teaches or suggests that little children
who die in infancy are ever lost. Moreover, Jesus says in
John 16 that the sin which condemns a man is the sin of
not believing on Jesus Christ. Since a child cannot accept
or reject, they have never committed the sin of rejecting
Jesus. Adam's sin was atoned for on the Cross, and there
is nothing at all in Scripture to indicate that any children
are ever lost. Jesus says, "it is not the will of your Father
which is in heaven, that one of these little ones should
perish" (Matthew 18:10, 14).

18. Are Baptism and the Lord's Supper for This Dispensation?

There are many of God's dear children who have difficulty placing baptism and the Lord's Supper in this dispensation. My personal belief is that the Lord's Supper is
for us now until He comes, and that baptism is our testimony to our death, burial and resurrection with the Lord
Jesus Christ through faith. However, the spirit of Chris-
tianity is that whether we agree or disagree on these points,
we can still love one another and unite in preaching the
Gospel of God's grace and then when we see Him, we shall
know all things plainly.

19. Is Infant Baptism Taught in the Bible?

I was born and raised in a church which taught and
practiced infant baptism and was the pastor of such a
church for four years. Carefully studying my Bible, I

found that infant baptism is nowhere taught or even suggested in the Scriptures. It is a doctrine of the church
which is certainly not founded upon the Word of God, but
is a remnant of Roman Catholicism. There is not a single
clear instance of it in the Bible, and no trace of it until
three hundred years after Pentecost. It is a wholly unscriptural doctrine of man. I would suggest that you limit
your studies more to the Scriptures rather than the doctrinal
standards of the church.

20. Is the Doctrine of Baptismal Regeneration Scriptural?

Regarding your question, Acts 2:38 and Acts 22:16 do
not teach baptismal regeneration. You will notice in
Acts 2:38 that repentance is mentioned first. Christ and
His apostles taught that baptism with water is an ordinance
to be obeyed as an outward testimony of an inward change
of heart, but they did not teach that one must be baptized
in order to be saved. In Acts 22:16 the passage has nothing
to do with the matter of water taking away sin. The
testimony of Paul is here to give witness to the fact that his
sins have been washed away. The literal rendering of this
passage is generally accepted as "Now why tarriest thou?
Arise and be baptized as thy sins are washed away, calling
on the Name of the Lord." The thief on the Cross never
was baptized. Please note Mark 16:16. This text does
not say, "He that is not baptized shall be damned (or
condemned)," but only "He that believeth not."

21. Does the Word, "Water," in John 3:5 Mean Baptism?

The word, "water," in John 3:5 refers to the Word of
God. This is very clear from the following Scriptures:
I Peter 1:23-24; Ephesians 5:26; John 17:17; and Titus
3:5. Symbolically in Scripture "water" speaks of the
"Word of God," and the teaching of John 3:5 is that we
are saved by the Spirit's application of the Word of God to

our hearts. See I John 5:10. The same is true of John
19:34.

22. Is the Lutheran Teaching of Baptism Scriptural?

I have read very carefully what you had to say concerning the Lutheran teaching of baptism. The teaching of
baptismal regeneration as taught by the Catholic and
Lutheran churches is a denial of the doctrine of salvation
by grace.

23. Who Should Be Baptized?

In regard to your question concerning baptism, let me
repeat that water baptism is not a saving ordinance, but
rather a blessed privilege on the part of God's children
as a testimony for Him. It is a privilege rather than a
command. In regard to I Corinthians 1:14, please note that
Paul definitely states that he *did* baptize some of the Corinthians, but because they made it such an issue, he was
thankful that he did not baptize any more of them.

I believe that a man must follow the leading of the
Holy Spirit in these matters. If God convicts us of the
need of baptism, we are disobedient if we refuse. However, I do not believe that anyone should be baptized who
does not fully desire in this way to witness for the Lord
Jesus Christ. Throughout the book of Acts, both Jews and
Gentiles were baptized as a testimony to their identification
to Christ. One can be saved without baptism, but to refuse
to be baptized makes one a disobedient believer.

24. Who Can Perform Baptism?

From the Scripture, there is no reason whatsoever to believe that a special clergyman or preacher must perform
baptism. Any born-again believer has the right to baptize
another. For the sake of order, I suppose the other method,
limiting the right to a certain class, was adopted.

25. What Is the Difference Between the Baptism of Peter and the Baptism of John?

In regard to your question concerning Acts 2:38, you must remember that at Pentecost all were Jews. There were no Gentiles there. This was still the baptism of repentance, the same baptism which John practised before the Cross. After Israel rejected the second offer of the Kingdom in Acts 7, the Gospel then goes to the Gentile, and we have Christian baptism which is quite different from John's baptism (See Acts 19:1-3) New Testament, Christian baptism is in the name of the Father, the Son and the Holy Spirit.

26. I Was Sprinkled As an Infant. Is It All Right for Me to Be Re-Baptized by Immersion?

In regard to your question concerning your re-baptism, I can understand your predicament quite thoroughly, since I too was brought up with a similar church background. I too was sprinkled as an infant, and then later the Lord saved my soul and showed me the truth about Bible baptism. I was re-baptized by immersion as my testimony of personal faith in the Lord Jesus Christ. Sprinkling is *not* baptism, and since I considered my so-called infant baptism as merely a dedication, I felt I must submit to immersion after I was saved. We do not believe that baptism adds to our salvation, or makes us fit for heaven. It is only our own personal testimony, and so all I can say is, you just follow the leading of the Lord and do as He convicts you. As far as I personally was concerned, I was re-baptized, but I am the last one to try to force my own convictions upon someone else.

27. Can There Be Another Pentecost? I Hear People Pray for Another Out-Pouring of the Holy Spirit. Is This Possible Today?

The answer to your question is both "no" and "yes."

There cannot be another out-pouring of the Holy Spirit *in this present* dispensation. The entire Holy Spirit was poured out personally on Pentecost and came in abiding presence on the Church, and cannot, therefore, be poured out until He is taken up with the Church in the rapture. Pentecost, however, was only a partial fulfillment of Joel chapter 3. The complete fulfillment of this prophecy will come only after the Church is gone. What we need, therefore, today is not another out-pouring of the Spirit, but a complete surrender and yielding to the already present, abiding indwelling Spirit of God.

28. Why Were the Disciples Baptized in the Name of Jesus?

The reason the disciples in the book of Acts (Acts 19:5) were baptized in the name of Jesus was because they were Jews. They already believed in the Father and the Spirit, but to be saved they had to acknowledge Jesus as God and a person of the Trinity. Hence, they were baptized in the name of Jesus, or Lord Jesus. Today, in this Gentile dispensation when we are to preach to all nations, the formula is "in the name of the Father, Son and Holy Spirit."

29. Is the Gift of Tongues for This Age?

We believe that according to I Corinthians 13, these special signs ceased when revelation (the Bible) was completed. It is not a matter of whether God is able to do these things, but entirely a matter of whether they are for this age and dispensation. Tongues together with other miracles were apostolic and ceased with the apostolic age.

30. Did the Signs and Gifts By Laying On of Hands Cease with the Apostolic Age?

We believe that the signs and gifts were committed by the Lord Jesus to the apostles and they were definitely apostolic gifts for the apostolic age only. In the New Testament, the apostles received these gifts, and they in turn were able to transfer these gifts by the laying on of hands to others as the Spirit directed. However, with them the signs and gifts ceased, and there is not a single instance in the Bible where anyone except the twelve apostles could transmit these gifts to others. Those upon whom they laid their hands could perform signs, but they were never able to give this to anyone else. It, therefore, passed with the death of the apostles, and so we believe that all who claim to have this apostolic gift today are frauds and deceivers.

31. Please Explain the Baptism of the Holy Spirit and Tongues To Me.

In regard to your question concerning the baptism of the Holy Spirit, we believe that every believer when he accepts the Lord Jesus Christ receives the baptism in the Holy Spirit and needs nothing more, except to grow in grace and in the knowledge of the Lord Jesus Christ.

I do not believe that the gift of tongues is for this present dispensation, and therefore, if we ask for more than just God's promise, we are asking for something with which the Lord is not pleased. I believe that there are many sincere people who believe in the work of "baptism" in the Holy Spirit and tongues, but I also believe that they are wrong, and not in harmony with the clear revelation of the Word of God.

CHAPTER 3

BIBLE

32. What Do You Think of the Different Bible Translations?

Many of the recent translations of the Bible are very
helpful for study and research, but there still has been no
translation of the Bible which can exceed the King James
Bible for accuracy.

33. Is Our Bible Complete?

In regard to your question, the books of the Bible as we
have them today complete the canon of Scripture. It is
very significant that our Lord Jesus Christ while He was
here on earth quoted from practically all of the books of
the Old Testament, from the books of Moses, the Psalms
and from the prophets, but never once did He quote from,
or recognize, any of the apocryphal books, including the
ones you mention, the books of Maccabees. This alone
proves that Jesus did not recognize these books as belonging
in the Bible.

34. What Are the So-Called "Lost Books" of the Bible?

In reality, there are no lost books of the Bible. We
believe the books contained in the present canon of
Scriptures are the ones the Holy Spirit directed to be in-
cluded. There are a number of other books mentioned
in Scripture which are lost, but these were not "inspired,"
or the Lord would have preserved them for us.

35. What Can We Say to Those Who Tell Us "You Can't Take the Bible Literally?"

The Bible should always be taken literally, except where the language is plainly symbolic, or where it is plainly stated that it is a parable or a type. In our common, every-day language we use figures of speech and have no trouble understanding them. We should read the Bible in the very same way. For instance, Jesus said, "I am the door." No one takes this to mean that He was a wooden door on hinges, but everyone understands that He is the only means of approach to God the Father. If we use the same common sense in reading the Bible which we do with our other reading, we will have no difficulty.

36. Someone Has Said, "The Bible Could Not Have Been Written in the Days of Moses, Because At That Time There Was No Writing." What Can We Tell Them?

If you have access to an encyclopedia, I would advise you to look up the history of the Tel El Amarna Tablets, which were written before the days of Moses, possibly as early as the days of Abraham. The old, modernistic objection which you quote has been long disproven.

37. What Is Your Opinion of the Concordant Version of the Bible?

I certainly do not recommend it. I believe that it contains gross error and is full of false teaching. Wherever it has gone, it has caused trouble and splitting and I have nothing good to say for the volume at all.

38. What Do You Think of the Weymouth Translation of the Bible?

Concerning the Weymouth translation of the New Testament, while I do not recommend it for general reading, I do find it very valuable and helpful in the study of the New Testament, alongside the King James version. I do not believe that any translation has yet been found which is as good as the King James, but many of them are helpful, and Weymouth's is one of these.

39. Someone Has Told Me That the New Translations of the Bible Have Been Printed To Suit the People. Is This True?

It is not true that the Bibles which we use today are printed in order to suit the people. Many of the new versions of the Bible I do not accept, since I do not believe that they are any improvement. Personally, I still believe that the best English translation is the old King James Version, which is still used by most Christians today. I know that there are a great many new versions, some of them by people who are partly modernistic. However, we believe that God has seen to it that His Word is protected against any serious error, and we know that His Holy Spirit is still able to illuminate those who are willing to do His will.

40. Do You Advise the Use of the Analytical Bible?

The Analytical Bible is a very fine piece of work and will be very helpful to those who wish to study the Bible more thoroughly. Personally, the most useful edition of the Bible is still the Scofield edition for my preaching and my general reading, but among other books I also use the new Analytical Bible, because I find that oftentimes it gives a great deal of information which is quite valuable. I do not believe that it will ever take the place of our Scofield Reference Bible, but it is a good addition to anyone's library, and I know that you will be much benefited by it.

41. Have You Read the Attack on the Scofield Bible?

In regard to the attack on the *Scofield Bible Notes*, I have not read all the attacks, but I am not surprised that some would attack these notes, since everyone does not agree with him. While I realize that Dr. Scofield was not infallible, and that he could not speak with final authority, I do praise God for his reference Bible which has been a mighty help to me in my understanding of the Scriptures, especially the truth of grace and the truth of the Second Coming of the Lord Jesus Christ. As far as his position on grace and law is concerned, I agree entirely with Dr. Scofield. I do not believe that we can mix law and grace. It is either one or the other. However, there will always be people who will disagree with God's servants, but when we get to heaven, we know that all of the blood-bought throng will agree in all things, and rejoice in the fellowship of the Lord Jesus Christ.

42. Do You Recommend the Use of the Chain Reference Bible?

I would not recommend it for daily use, but only as a reference Bible for the sake of study, for those who want to dig into the various truths of the Word of God from every conceivable angle.

43. Someone Told Me That the Bible Contained Fables. Is this True?

In regard to your question as to whether there are fables in the Bible, this depends entirely upon the definition of a fable. Of course, we know that there are many parables in the Bible, and they are called "parables," but I believe that it is best that we do not call them fables. A parable, as you know, is an illustration in order to clarify some other truth and as such they are perfectly legitimate. Jesus used many parables in His teaching. I would not want to say that they are fables, however; but rather call them parables.

44. How Many Gospels Are There Mentioned in Scripture?
There are a number of "gospels" mentioned in the Scriptures. First of all, there is the "kingdom" gospel, which was the offer of the kingdom to Israel. This was rejected at His first coming, but will be accepted when He comes again. Then there is the "gospel of the grace of God" which refers to this dispensation as contrasted with the law. Paul also calls this "my gospel." Then in Revelation, we have the "everlasting gospel" which is the message of the kingdom which will be proclaimed during the tribulation period. However, they are all the gospel of grace, since it is God's offer to unworthy recipients, and so in reality there is only one gospel with a different emphasis in different dispensations.

CHAPTER 4

BIBLE CHARACTERS

45. In Studying Hebrews, Chapter 11, I Notice That Adam's Name Was Not Mentioned Among the Other Faithful Old Testament Saints, and I Am Wondering If Adam Was Saved?

In regard to your question in Hebrews 11, concerning the omission of the name of Adam from the register of faith in this chapter, this omission means nothing for two reasons: first, there are many other names of Old Testament saints omitted, as well. And second, Genesis 3:21 tells us definitely that God clothed Adam with the skin of the sacrifice which God Himself provided. "Unto Adam also and to his wife did the Lord God make coats of skins, and clothed them" (Gen. 3:21). This settles for me Adam's salvation. Anyone who is clothed with God's covering must be saved.

46. Did Adam Know the Way of Salvation Before He Fell?

There can be no question that Adam knew the heart and mind of God far better before he fell than after. How much he knew of the plan of salvation, I do not know, but he understood God's holiness which demanded death, and also understood that a kinsman redeemer was required.

47. Was the Fruit Which Adam and Eve Took From the Forbidden Tree Literal Fruit and a Literal Tree, Or Is This Used Symbolically?

Concerning the sin of Adam and Eve and the tree of knowledge, we must accept the whole thing as literal. If it were not a literal tree, then it was not a literal woman, and then it could not have been a literal Adam. The whole story must be taken literally. God had placed man on the earth and God was sovereign because He had created him. As a sovereign God, He had a right to put man to the test and so He forbade him just the eating of this one single tree. By the act of eating, Adam showed that he rebelled against the will of God. Please remember that he was in a garden filled with all the fruits which his heart could desire, but still he went contrary to the will of God. I am sure that if we take the whole thing literally, we will have no difficulty whatsoever.

48. If Abraham Was Sterile, How Could He Be the Father of Ishmael?

In regard to your question concerning Abraham, I am very glad that you brought it up, because it all adds to the miracle of God's wonder-working power. As far as Ishmael was concerned, you must remember that Ishmael was born thirteen years before Isaac was born. Evidently, therefore, Abraham was still able to produce a seed at that particular age with the bondwoman Hagar from Egypt, but according to Romans, when Isaac was born, Abraham's body was as good as dead as far as having children was concerned. Moreover, we know also that Sarah had long passed the age of child-bearing. This makes the birth of Isaac a supernatural miracle as a result of God's intervention.

The fact that Abraham later married Keturah and had six more children only adds to the thoroughness of God's work. God evidently revived Abraham's body supernaturally so that he could become the father of Isaac, and the work that God did was not only temporary, but continued many years afterward, so that he was even able to have children with his third wife.

49. Was Abraham a Jew or Gentile?

Abraham was a Gentile until God called him and he came to Palestine. Then he was called a Hebrew. The Jews were only called such after the captivity into Babylon. The name, "Jew," comes from "Judah" and refers to a member of the Southern Kingdom of Judah. Abraham was not an Israelite, not a Jew, but a Hebrew.

50. What Is the Significance of Eve's Creation from the Rib of Adam?

Eve was made from Adam's side as a type of the wounded side of Christ, from which the blood and the water flowed in the making up of the Bride of Christ, the Church.

51. Was Esau Lost or Saved?

There is no doubt that Esau was lost because he despised his birthright. Esau was the eldest brother in the family of Isaac. Therefore, he was in the line of the promised seed of the Lord Jesus Christ which was to run through Abraham, Isaac and Jacob, and then on until Christ should come. Since the line of the seed ran through Isaac, the father of Esau, he being the first-born, would be in line of becoming an ancestor of the promised seed. This is all implied in his birthright. Since he despised it, he cast aside the one to whom the birthright pointed, namely, the Lord Jesus Christ, and this rejection was the sin that caused Esau to repent, and yet to find no repentance later on. Jacob, although no better than Esau, and probably much more shady in his dealings, valued the birthright and by it was justified in the sight of God.

52. Was Judas Saved and Later Lost? From the Example of Judas It Seems That It Would Be Possible to Fall from Salvation. It This So?

In regard to Judas, we are told not that he fell from

salvation, but he fell from his apostleship, which is quite another thing. I personally do not believe that Judas was ever saved.

53. What If Judas Had Not Betrayed Christ?

I see your difficulty quite thoroughly. We must distinguish between God's sovereign plan and human responsibility. In the eternal plan of God He already knew everyone who would be saved, and who would not be saved. This, of course, includes Judas as well. Judas came into the world for this very purpose, just as God raised up Pharaoh in the days of Israel in order that He might destroy him. You will find this very definitely taught in the 9th, 10th and 11th chapters of Romans which I suggest that you read. I realize that there are many of these things which are deep, and we cannot understand them until we meet Him face to face. In the meantime let us continue to study the Word of God for further light, since none of us are as yet perfect. There is no question in my mind but that Judas was the instrument of Satan for the betrayal of Christ, in the eternal purpose of God. Of course, when we say, "If Judas had not betrayed the Lord Jesus Christ, so and so would not have happened," we must take into consideration that God knew that he would betray the Lord Jesus. Therefore, it was all according to plan.

54. Will Judas Be the Antichrist?

In regard to your question concerning the Man of Sin, there is no direct statement in the Bible that it will be Judas who will be raised from the dead, but we do know that the same name is applied to him which is applied to the antichrist. In the book of Revelation, chapter 13, we are told that the beast will give life to the image of the beast. That is, that he will cause it to be resurrected. Of course, we are not too dogmatic about these matters of Judas, but it does look very much, since he is the imitation of the true Christ, that he will be the one whom Satan will tempt once more to oppose the Lord Jesus Christ when He comes again. The only two persons in the Bible called "son of perdition" are the antichrist and Judas. We, therefore, believe they are the same.

55. Is There a Bible Record of John the Baptist's Conversion?

In regard to your question concerning John the Baptist, the Bible does not record the account of his conversion. The Scripture in Luke 1:15, "For he shall be great in the sight of the Lord, and shall drink neither wine nor strong drink; and he shall be filled with the Holy Ghost," has to do with John's mission as the forerunner of Christ, rather than with his conversion. According to God's foreknowledge, all His children are foreknown and predestined from eternity. Luke 1:15 should be looked at in this light. God predestines all His children even from before the foundation of the world (Ephesians 1:4).

56. Someone Told Me That the Book of Job Was the Oldest Book in the Bible. I Always Thought That Job Lived After Abraham. Can You Give Me Some Help On This Matter?

Let me put your mind at rest by saying that it is not my own personal opinion alone, that Job lived probably before the days of Abraham, but this is the consensus of practically all Bible scholars and Bible students. The content of the book of Job, the fact that he lived over two hundred years, and many other things, indicate clearly that Job probably lived before Abraham. The book may not have been written until a later time by some other author, such as Moses, but it is generally agreed by those who have made a study of this book that Job is a character antedating the days of Abraham.

57. Who Is Melchizedek?

There are several theories concerning the identity of Melchizedek. Some believe that he was Shem, the son of Noah. Others believe that he was a type of the Lord Jesus Christ, while still other teachers believe that he was actually the Lord Jesus Himself. There is great disagreement among Bible students as to this mysterious personage. Personally, I believe that he was a *type* of the Lord Jesus Christ.

58. I Heard You Make the Statement That Moses Would Be One of the Witnesses Mentioned in Revelation 11. I Cannot Reconcile This With the Fact That Moses Had Already Died.

I am quite familiar with the objections usually raised against including Moses among the two witnesses of Revelation 11. The entire objection stems from the statement in Hebrews 9:27, that it is appointed unto men "once to die." This, however, is spoken of the race generically, and does not refer to each and every individual. In I Corinthians 15:51 we read that we shall not all sleep. There will be many people at the second coming of Christ who will never see death. Evidently, if some are never to die, the verse in Hebrews 9:27 is spoken in a general sense, not individual.

59. Someone Told Me That It Took Noah 120 Years to Build the Ark, But I Have Been Unable to Find This Statement in the Bible. Is It Correct That It Took Him That Long to Build the Ark?

I feel that you are perfectly correct in your statement that there is no evidence in the Bible that Noah was 120 years building the Ark, or that he preached for 120 years. This erroneous deduction, is gathered from the fact that God said to Noah that the years of grace before the coming of the flood would be 120 years. However, there is no

positive proof that Noah was this length of time in building the Ark.

60. Were Either Nebuchadnezzar or Darius Saved?

There seems to be no question whatsoever from the
record in Daniel that Nebuchadnezzar was truly converted. Of course, he had never yet heard of the Lord
Jesus Christ as such, because He had not yet been born, but
by faith in the Word of God, as they had it then, he was
undoubtedly converted.

As to Darius, we are not so sure. Bible students are not
agreed as to his actual conversion. The Bible does indicate, however, that he was used of the Lord for the carrying out of His program, but as to his actual conversion, the
Bible seems to be silent.

61. Concerning Pharaoh, What Does It Mean in Exodus Where It Keeps Mentioning That "God Hardened Pharaoh's Heart"?

In regard to your question concerning the hardening of
Pharaoh's heart, there are two things which must be
remembered. First of all, it must be read in the light of
Romans 9:17, where it is definitely said that God raised
up Pharaoh for the very purpose of which the book of
Exodus tells us. It was that He might show His power in
him. This refers to the sovereignty of God. On the other
hand, we must remember that in the book of Exodus we
have at least three different stages in the hardening of
Pharaoh's heart. First of all, we read in Exodus 8:15
that "Pharaoh hardened his heart." In Exodus 9:7 we
read, "and the heart of Pharaoh was hardened," and in
Exodus 9:12 we have the record, "and the Lord hardened
the heart of Pharaoh." I believe that we have to look at
it in two ways. First of all, that God did in sovereign
power harden the heart of Pharaoh, but as far as he was

concerned, he first hardened his own heart. Then his heart was hardened, and finally, God hardened his heart.

62. Was Saul Saved?

Saul was never saved. God came upon him and gave him power for being king, but not to salvation. Saul died an unbelieving suicide.

63. Was Solomon a Saved Man?

Concerning Solomon, there is no doubt about the fact that Solomon was saved, but undoubtedly he lost much of his reward. He was chosen of the Lord and a type of the Lord Jesus Christ in His kingdom glory, so while his life ended rather obscurely and tragically, we do believe that God's grace is greater than all of our sins, and while Solomon stands as an example of how a man greatly used of the Lord may finally get out of fellowship, we do believe that he was saved. God is the Judge in these things and these are only our opinions.

CHAPTER 5

BLOOD

64. Does Our Family Background and Ancestry Decrease or Increase Our Possibility of Sinning?

In regard to your question concerning the blood and the possibility of sinning, you must not forget that according to Romans 3 and Psalm 14, all men are equally lost and sinful, but all do not manifest that sin externally in the same degree. Environment, education, fear of punishment and many other factors we have to restrain the expression of sin, but the picture in Romans 3 is the picture of every human heart, and a child does not get any of this from the mother, but all of it way back from father Adam, the same place where the mother got it.

65. Is There a Difference in the Blood of the Different Races?

Science has definitely proven that there is no difference whatsoever between the blood of the Negro and the white, the yellow and the red. The difference is entirely a matter of external appearance caused by environment and climatic conditions over many generations. The blood of a Negro works just as well in transfusions of white people as colored folks. The blood is the same in all. Paul already expressed this nineteen hundred years ago in Acts 17:26. Science has just found out what Paul knew almost two thousand years ago.

66. Should We Eat Blood in This Dispensation?

It is wrong for us to eat blood today as well as things strangled. Kosher meat as butchered according to the law is considered by health experts far superior to or-

48

dinary butchered meat. However, when meat is butchered in the regular way and thoroughly drained of its blood, it is perfectly fit to eat. Although some of the fluid of the blood may be there, it is the principle that counts rather than some amount of undrainable blood. The prohibition against eating blood was given before the law (Genesis 9:4), and repeated after the law was fulfilled in Christ (Acts 15:20).

67. If the Blood Is Contributed to the Child By the Father, How Is It Possible for a Child to Resemble Its Mother?

The parental traits and resemblances of a child to its parents are determined at the time of conception when the male and female genes come together. It is a matter of genetics, *not* of blood. The mother contributes the nutritive elements, anti-bodies, the fluids and all the elements that make up the tissues, but no actual tissue cells.

It must be borne in mind that while no actual blood passes from mother to child, that the elements (nutritive), chemical bodies, anti-bodies and anti-toxins do pass from mother to child, and the body substances are transferred, not through the actual blood, but through the contents of the blood.

68. Is Christ's Blood in Heaven Today?

In regard to your question concerning I John 5:7-8, there is no direct statement that the blood is literally in heaven, but since His blood is incorruptible according to Scripture, it must be somewhere, since it cannot be destroyed. As the High Priest in heaven, the Lord Jesus Christ would logically have the blood there.

69. Can Blood Tests Prove Parentage?

In answer to your question concerning the positive blood chemistry test to prove parentage, there is no "positive" test, although today it is accepted as quite reliable. I suggest that you see your physician in regard to any problems that you may have in mind.

70. What Is Your Opinion of Selling Blood for the Blood Bank?

In regard to your question concerning giving of blood, I believe the matter of accepting remuneration for donating blood is a matter of individual personal decision. I personally would not care to receive any remuneration or money for blood that I might give in order to help some other suffering member of humanity. I should feel much better to give this freely as a service in the name of the Lord Jesus Christ.

71. Why Do the Genealogies of Christ Differ in Matthew and Luke?

Matthew gives the genealogy of Jesus Christ from David through Solomon, David's son, and up to Joseph. Luke gives the genealogy of Jesus Christ from Adam to David, then through Nathan and up to Heli, the father of Mary. You will notice that Matthew gives the genealogy of Joseph, and Luke gives the genealogy of Mary. Both are descendants of David, of course. Jesus Christ had to be legal heir to the Throne and as the line does not run through the woman but through the man, Jesus had to be the foster son of a man in David's line.

72. Was the Resurrection Body of the Lord Jesus Christ Bloodless?

I do not believe that the Lord Jesus' body was bloodless. I believe that every drop of His blood still exists. When He died on the Cross, we are told at least four times that He cried with a loud voice, which would preclude the possibility of His dying from hemorrhage. The idea of a bloodless body is suggested by the fact that Jesus said to His disciples, "For a spirit hath not flesh and bones, as ye see Me have" (Luke 24:39). However, this does not necessarily mean that He had no blood. Then the verse, "Flesh and blood shall not inherit the kingdom of heaven" (I Cor. 15:50), does not mean that blood shall not be in heaven, but rather that flesh and blood as we see it today in its sinful form shall have no place in heaven. The blood of Jesus was not "spilled," but *shed* for us.

73. If a Child Receives Its Blood from the Father, How Do You Account For the Fact That It Does Not Always Have the Same Blood Type?

It isn't necessary that the child have the same type of blood as the father. A child may develop any one of the four different types. The point is this — that if a child received its blood from its mother directly, it would have to be the same type, which is not the case, whereas the unborn child develops its own blood within its own system. As a result of the paternal principle, it may be any one of the different types. The type of blood is transmitted by the parental genes at conception and not during its development.

74. Are Human and Animal Blood the Same?

Human blood and animal blood are not the same. God breathed life into Adam, but not into animals. An animal has a soul but no spirit.

CHAPTER 6

CHRIST

75. Does the Resurrection Body of Christ Bear the Scars of His Wounds?

Yes, according to Luke 23:39 and Zechariah 13:6, the resurrection body of Jesus retains the wounds of Calvary. Since it was a resurrection body, and therefore, perfect, I assume the wounds were healed and the scars alone remain.

76. Was Christ's Body Broken?

In regard to the breaking of the body of the Lord Jesus Christ, we must remember that while not a *bone* of His body was broken, His body itself was broken in many places by the scourging, the crown of thorns and the nails in the hands and feet. To say that His body was broken does not in any way imply that His bones were broken. (See John 19:33, 36)

77. Could Jesus Sin?

In regard to your question concerning Christ's ability to sin, we must remember that Christ was both God and man. As God He could not sin, since deity cannot sin. As a man, however, He was subject to all temptations and He could have listened to the devil if He had chosen to. However, He proved by not sinning, that He was greater than the devil even as a man. Also, He proved that Adam had no excuse for sinning, for if he had met the tempter just as the last Adam did, he would not have fallen.

78. Was Jesus Tested or Tempted?

Yes, Jesus as the Son of Man and a human was tested and tempted as we are. As deity, Jesus could not be tempted, for "God cannot be tempted, neither doth He tempt any man." If you will read the record of His temptation in Luke, you will recognize He met Satan as a perfect Man, and not as the Son of God. The force of Satan's temptation was this, that he tried to get Jesus to use His deity and came each time with "If Thou be the Son of God," but Jesus met him as a man and conquered him as a man.

79. How Could Jesus Be Tempted in All Points Like As We Are?

Jesus was the last Adam and the Second Man. As such He could be tempted just as Adam was before he received his sinful nature. The only difference is that Adam yielded and Jesus overcame.

80. Did Christ Have An Occupation Before He Entered His Public Ministry?

It is usually supposed that Jesus was a carpenter, because the Pharisees said in Mark 6:3, "Is not this the carpenter, the son of Mary?" We must remember that while He was Divine and God, He was also human. He certainly was a Priest and a King, but He was also One who became like unto us in *all* things.

81. Why Was Christ Baptized?

In regard to your question concerning the baptism of Christ, the Scripture says this was done to fulfill all righteousness. It was to identify Himself with the people whom He came to save that Christ was baptized, although He had no sin. It was His declaration of willingness to go through death and resurrection for His people.

82. Why Didn't Jesus Know the Day or Hour That He Would Come Again?

In regard to your question concerning the words of Jesus that no one knows the day nor hour (Mark 13:32), you must remember that Christ here was speaking as the Son of Man. As the Son of God He knows all things. As the Son of Man, He was subject to the limitations of our humanity. The only way to understand this is to remember that Christ was both man and God, and this statement in Mark refers to His manhood, not His deity.

83. Did Jesus Have Brothers and Sisters?

I suggest that you read carefully Matthew 13, verses 55 and 56, which establishes beyond doubt the fact that Mary had children, both boys and girls, after the birth of Christ. Jesus was the firstborn, but the very fact that He had natural brothers and sisters establishes the fact that He became flesh of our flesh and bone of our bone.

84. Did Jesus Die As Deity or Man?

Jesus was man in that He bore our sins in His own body on the tree. However, He was also God, since no man was able to pay the infinite penalty of sin. The fact that Jesus made full payment in the brief space of six hours proves that it was the *man* Jesus who paid the penalty to satisfy deity.

85. Why Was Christ Sold for Thirty Pieces of Silver?

Thirty shekels of silver in the time of Christ amounted to about three pounds and fifteen shillings in English money. This was the price of a slave in Israel. (See Exodus 21:32.) At the rate of $5.00 to a pound, this would be $18.75. However, you must realize that the value of a pound fluctuates, at present being slightly less than $5. It might be interesting to you to notice that Joseph was sold for twenty shekels which in English money would be two pounds and ten shillings, or $12.50 in our money. This low price was due to the fact that he was only a lad and not a full-grown slave.

86. Did Jesus Ever Laugh?

There is no record in the Bible that Jesus ever laughed or smiled. I do not say that He never smiled, but simply that the Bible does not record that He ever did.

87. What Is the Significance of the "Water and Blood" From Christ's Side When He Was Pierced on the Cross By the Soldier?

It is a well-known, scientific fact that when people die from a violent death and the heart stops, the blood collects on the left side and begins to separate into the serum and the solid elements of blood, such as the corpuscles, etc. Whenever blood separates in the body it is a scientific proof of death. Hence the blood and the water speak of the death of Christ, scientifically authenticated, so that the theory that Christ only swooned is absolutely disproven.

88. On What Day Was Christ Crucified, and on What Day Did He Arise?

It is my firm conviction that Christ was crucified on Wednesday, and arose right after sundown on Saturday night, which was the beginning of the first day in the Jewish calendar. In no other way can we account for three days and three nights. "Good Friday" is an unscriptural tradition only.

89. Why Is Christ's Robe Described As Scarlet in Matthew and Purple in the Other Gospels?

In regard to the fact that the gospels speak of the purple robe, while in Matthew we have a scarlet robe, I think you will understand when I give you the meaning of the words. The word for "purple" in the Greek is "prophura," and means literally, "a red-blue" color. As you know, the combination of red and blue make purple. The word used in Matthew for "scarlet" is "kakkinos," and means not only scarlet, but means generally "a colored garment," so we may read in the gospels that they put upon Him a red-blue garment, while Matthew says that they put upon Him a colored garment, which might be the same thing, and in this case undoubtedly was.

90. Was Christ Born in a Stable or in a Manger?

In regard to your question concerning the birthplace of the Lord Jesus Christ, the word, "stable," is not used in the account, but we are told that Jesus was "laid in a manger." A manger is a feeding trough for cattle, and it is generally assumed that He was born in a place where the cattle were fed. I realize that ofttimes these feeding places were outside and not in a building. Whatever the place may have been, it was a place which served as a feeding place for animals and this is usually considered to be a stable. You will find the record of this in the second chapter of Luke. Jesus was born in the stable and then laid in the manger.

91. Someone Told Me That the Reason Christ Sweat Drops of Blood Was That He Feared Satan Would Kill Him. Is This According to the Teaching of God's Word?

I do not find anything in the entire Bible for that kind of theory. I would rather believe that the suffering of Christ was because He became our sin-bearer in Gethsemane and bore our sins to the Cross of Calvary. Jesus did not fear death; He feared only sin and it was our sins which the Lord, according to Isaiah 53:6, laid upon Him as the Son of God, which caused this great agony.

Moreover, the Bible does not say that He sweat blood, but it distinctly says, that He sweat "as it were" great drops of blood, falling down to the ground (Luke 22:44).

I am afraid that these theories are stretching the Word of God beyond its apparent meaning. However, we do appreciate the sufferings of Christ in our behalf, and when we get to glory we will understand some of the agony through which He had to pass in our behalf.

92. Where in the Bible Does It State That "The Angel of the Lord" Always Refers to the Lord Jesus Christ in the Old Testament?

There is no direct statement which says in so many exact words that the "angel of the Lord" is always the Lord Jesus, but it is rather on the accumulation of evidence where the term occurs in Scripture. From the various passages where the expression, "the angel of the Lord," occurs, it is quite evident that it is the second Person of the Trinity who is there and who is the spokesman for the Trinity itself. We call this a "theophany," or an appearing of the Lord Jesus Christ in human form before His incarnation in Bethlehem. As is true of other doctrines of Scripture, we cannot put our finger on any one particular passage which states in so many words that this is true, but we have to assume it from the revelation. There is no verse in the Bible which says in so many words that God is a "trinity" consisting of one God and three Persons, but there are enough passages which indicate this very clearly so that we can form a doctrine of the Trinity on it.

93. Does the Bible Say Anything About Making or Having Pictures of Christ?

In regard to your question about what the Bible has to say concerning making pictures of objects, and especially of Christ or His disciples, we cannot find any positive

scriptures. In the Law of Moses, the Israelite was forbidden to make any image or likeness of anything in
heaven, or the earth below, or the waters under the earth.
Now the real purpose of this was the making of pictures
with the idea of worshipping them, and the law goes on to
say, "Thou shalt not bow down thyself to them, nor worship
them." The sin lies not in making the picture, but in the
worshipping of the image of the picture. Of course, we do
not know what the Lord Jesus Christ looked like while He
was here on earth.

94. Why Was Christ Born in Bethlehem?

God in His own foreknowledge ordained when and where
His own Son should be born. From the very beginning the
religious leaders of Jesus' day rejected Him, and it is wonderful to know that even as "Jesus came to seek and save
that which was lost," His birth could be announced to
humble shepherds.

95. Was Christ Buried on the Jewish Passover Sabbath Day, or the Day Before, To Make It a Full Three Days and Nights? He Did Observe the Passover with His Disciples.

The Passover occurred on the fourteenth day of the
first month. To this rule there was only one exception in
the days of Hezekiah in II Chronicles 30. The Passover
Lamb was prepared on the day before the Passover, usually
called the Passover Eve. This would make it the 13th day
of the month. Since the Passover was one of Israel's
national holidays, Christ would have to be sacrificed on the
Passover Eve and remained in the tomb on the 14th,
15th and 16th days of Abib, corresponding to our April,
and arose on April 17th, three days later.

CHAPTER 7

CHRISTIAN CONDUCT

96. What Do You Think of Nurses Working on Sunday?

The Lord understands that we are in a world which does not recognize Christ or the Word. Certainly there can be no harm in working on Sunday as long as it is an act of mercy and a necessity. Christ also healed on the Sabbath Day.

97. Many Times I Am Unable To Take the Opportunity I Have of Speaking for the Lord. As a Christian Nurse It Is My Desire to Serve the Lord, But We Are Not Permitted to Discuss Religion While on Duty. What Can I do?

I fully realize the difficulty which many nurses encounter in certain institutions where they are forbidden to talk about spiritual things. However, you can live the life of Christ before them and you can pray for them. When off duty you can distribute Christian literature and talk to folks outside for Christ.

98. Should Christians Vote?

In regard to your voting question, I believe that the Christian is a pilgrim here, but while he is here, he is subject to the laws of the land through which he travels. Since the powers that be are ordained of God, and we must subject ourselves to every ordinance of man, I believe that the Christian should vote.

When our house catches fire we call the fire department and when we are robbed we call the police. We need these governmental protections and there can be no harm in voting for them.

99. Should Christians Own Property?

In answering this question, we must remember that the incident in Acts, chapters 2 and 4, was during a time of great persecution and when the Church was still in possession of the Kingdom truth, but not the full truth of the Church. It is true that we should not make our homes and our possessions our idols, but I do believe that we should make proper provision for our loved ones. Remember that Paul says in I Timothy 5:8 — "But if any provide not for his own, and specially for those of his own house, he hath denied the faith, and is worse than an infidel."

100. What Should I Tell My Child about Santa Claus?

I quite appreciate the problem which is facing you. In the face of all the tradition and what everyone else believes, it is not an easy matter. However, there is only one thing to do and we have followed it with our children. We have told them the truth, and explained that Santa Claus is merely a myth, not a reality.

101. What Do You Think of Having a Christmas Tree?

The custom of having Christmas trees is of pagan origin, carried over by the Catholic church from paganism and adopted by the Protestants. Originally it was intended to represent the immortality of the pagan god, Tammuz, mentioned in Ezekiel 8:14. Personally, I do not believe that such symbols have any place at all in our Christian worship.

102. Are Christians Forbidden to Eat Pork?

This is clearly answered in the Bible. If you will read carefully the tenth chapter of Acts concerning the sheet that was let down from heaven, you will find the answer to your question. Since Calvary, the old ceremonial laws are fulfilled, and there are no restrictions as to clean and unclean meat.

I would suggest that you read also Acts 11:5-10. There Peter was commanded to eat foods unclean according to the law; however, if you have any conscientious scruples against it, read I Corinthians 8:7, 8, 9. If your conscience troubles you, or if your physical condition is such that you cannot stand pork, the thing to do is not to eat it. Scripturally, there is no prohibition against it. "Let every man be persuaded in his own mind." We are called to liberty, not contention.

103. What Should Be the Christian's Attitude Toward the Laws of the Land?

The Bible is quite clear that Christians are supposed to be subject to the powers that be and to submit themselves to every ordinance of man as a testimony. I must confess to you, that with the multiplicity of laws, regulations and restrictions, it is becoming more and more difficult to know just where to stop. Where the law does not interfere with our free worship of God, I believe we should do all we can to obey. When the law interferes with our duty to God, "we ought to obey God rather than man."

104. Are Christians Permitted To Cast Lots?

In regard to casting lots, if it is done seeking to know the will of the Lord, and not for gambling or gain, I think the Bible permits it. It is only to be used, however, where the Lord's will is not definitely known.

105. Are Christians Permitted to Use Strong Drink?

Personally, I believe that because of the evil effects of drink, and the definite warnings in the Bible against strong drink, a Christian should refrain from using it, even though he may be able to use it moderately. The path of safety always lies on the conservative side.

106. Do You Think That a Christian Should Work in the Home and Around the House on Sunday?

Your question concerning work on the Lord's Day is one that depends in part upon the environment in which you live, as well as your own conscience. I believe that, while the Bible does not give commandment concerning one day a week, it is a principle that the Christian set aside the first day of the week for Christian fellowship, assembling together, breaking of bread and prayer. I would advise you to find some other way to take care of your garden. It might injure your testimony if others saw you doing this, and we need at least one day a week when our bodies can rest, and we can apply ourselves to spiritual things particularly.

107. Who Should Ask Grace in the Home?

In regard to your question concerning asking grace, the head of the house should be the leader in this. He should use his own words and if you have visitors whom you know are Christians, it is perfectly proper also to ask them to say grace. It is a good custom to allow each member of the family to take their turns at this.

108. Can a Person Be Saved and Still Smoke?

There are better uses to which to put one's money, than to burn it up. However, to make it a condition of salvation is quite another thing. I have known many sincere Christians who did not seem to be convicted of this particular thing as sin. I think it is dangerous to judge one in regard to any habit. It is better to pray for them that the

Lord may convict them of the offence that these things often make in the lives of others. The principle laid down by Paul in I Corinthians 8 should be our guide in these matters.

109. Should Christians Observe Lent?

In regard to your question concerning Lent, I am sorry to say that this is nothing else but a Roman Catholic tradition without any proof or foundation in the Scriptures whatsoever. The well-informed Christian who knows the Word pays no attention to Lent whatsoever.

110. My Job Necessitates My Working on Sunday, and I Have Become Concerned about This Matter. Can You Help Me in Regard to This Problem?

In regard to working on Sunday, we must remember that no one can judge the other. There are certain occupations in which Sunday work is unavoidable. Farmers, electrical workers, hospital workers and many others find some Sunday work necessary. I do not believe that one can make a rule, but that every one should be persuaded in his own mind. Where it is necessary, and in the interest of safety and public health, I believe that Sunday work is unavoidable, and therefore, permissible. I certainly would not want to go on record as telling a man to give up his livelihood because of a certain amount of Sunday work. My advice to you is to pray about it, and if it is the Lord's will for you not to work on Sunday, I am sure He will open up something which will not make it necessary.

111. I Am Interested in Learning Your Opinion on the Use of Tobacco, Both From the Stand-Point of a Physician and a Bible Teacher.

The question which you raise in regard to the use of tobacco is one which has been raised by a great many Christians in these days. The medical profession seems to be divided somewhat as to the real ill effect of the use of tobacco upon the human system, but this is probably due to the fact that most physicians themselves are users of tobacco in some form or another. There can be no question whatsoever but that the excessive use of tobacco in any form is harmful to the human system, both physically and to the nervous system. For this reason almost all physicians advise against the use of it in the treatment of many physical diseases. This in itself is evidence that it is harmful to many of the organs of the body, especially when used in excessive quantities. However, I believe that the argument should rest upon a different ground than the mere effects upon the human body.

I feel that there are two reasons which should be given against its use. First, it is offensive to a great many other people, and as Christians we should seek to remove any offence in our own lives against others. Paul, you remember, said he would eat no meat while the earth standeth, if this eating of meat would be an offence to any of his weaker brethren. For this reason those things in our lives should be eliminated which in any way hinder others from being their best for the Lord. The second reason against its use is that there are other ways in which money can be spent where it will do a great deal more good than merely using it for this habit. Of course, those who use it claim that it gives them a certain amount of satisfaction, and comes under the heading of pleasure, but I do believe that the money spent for the use of tobacco as well as many other pleasures which even Christians enjoy, might be better used for the propagation of the Gospel, and for the spreading of the good news of salvation. As to the best way of overcoming the habit, there are many cures which promise to rid the addict of every desire for its use. Many of these have utterly failed, and I believe that only complete trust in the delivering power of the Lord Jesus Christ is able to help us to overcome any habit.

However, we must remember that we should not preach legalism to the unsaved. I do not believe in talking to people who are not born again about their personal habits. We should press upon them the need of salvation and of the new birth, and then permit the Lord to convict them of those things which are displeasing in their lives.

112. How Should We Observe the First Day of the Week?

The sabbath was indeed a time of absolute rest, while our first day of the week is resurrection day, and there-fore, a day of activity, the exact opposite of rest. The Sabbath speaks of death; the Lord's Day speaks of life. Our Saviour spent the Sabbath in the tomb, but He spent the first day of the week in ceaseless activity appearing to the women, the disciples and to the eleven in the evening. Instead of the first day of the week being a day of laziness and inactivity, we should spend it in the ceaseless business of worshipping the Lord, telling of His grace and winning souls for Christ. This is the reason that the word, sabbath, should never be applied to the first day of the week, the Lord's Day.

113. Should Christians Save from Their earnings for Old Age?

The Lord wants us to make provision for our family. "He that provideth not for his own is worse than a heathen," says Paul to Timothy (I Timothy 5:8), and reasonable business wisdom is legitimate among Christians, for while we are "not of the world, we are in the world." However, we are not to set our hearts upon these things.

114. What Do You Think of a Christian Charging Interest on Money Loaned, In The Light of Psalm 15:5?

The word, "usury," in Scriptures means "the charging of excessive money for the use of money loaned." Among Christians, I believe we should not charge interest, but give to those who are in need freely, and as Jesus says, without expecting return. In business, however, you understand it is almost impossible to compete without competitive methods which necessitate the loaning and borrowing of money. We are in the world but not of the world and there are some things we cannot avoid. We believe that a distinction should be made between our dealings with Christians and with those of the world.

115. Should a Christian Go to War?

The attitude of the Christian toward war is an extremely difficult one. We know that war is of the devil and that we are called to peace. However, we are in the world, though not of the world, and we are also admonished to be obedient to the powers that be. While the sole principle of war is contrary to the teachings of Christ, we must nevertheless witness for Christ by being obedient to the laws of the land. However, I do believe that the matter is one of individual, personal conscience, and as you know, our government recognizes those who are conscientious objectors. This, I believe, is about as far as we can go in stating the Biblical attitude towards war in this dispensation.

116. Should a Christian Carry Life Insurance?

Your question concerning life insurance is often raised among Christians. However, I do not see any difference between investing in insurance or putting money in the bank. Certainly we should not live for money, but the Lord does expect that we shall provide for our loved ones.

This applies to fire insurance and all other types. However, it is a matter of individual conscience.

117. I Have Received Some Literature Concerning Nudism Which Sets Forth the Idea That This Is the Way God Intended for Us to Live. I Would Like Your View on This Matter.

A detailed discussion of nudism is not possible by mail, but I can give you my view in a very few words. I believe that nudism is a thing of the devil, and has no place at all in our Christian living. It is entirely a physical thing and certainly has no substantiation in the Word of God. From what I have read about nudism, it is a disgrace and has no moral benefit or physical help of any kind.

118. Can a Christian Scripturally Swear to an Oath?

This again is a matter of individual privilege. The law of the land recognizes the right of an individual for conscientious reasons to refuse to take an oath. For this reason, anyone having objections is not compelled to do so. As for Scripture, many people use James 5:12, but at the same time, the Bible also records many instances of the taking of oaths to confirm a testimony.

119. Please Give Me Your Opinion on Christians Having Television.

In regard to your question concerning television, I have some very deep convictions concerning this matter, and personally I think it is much more of an evil than it is of good or of blessing. It is the most expensive way of getting the Gospel out. The cost of television is so tremendous that we could reach far more people by radio than we can by television. Moreover, I believe that "faith cometh by hearing," and not by seeing.

There is so much trash on television that I would not

have one in my home at all. Especially where there are small children, I think it is an evil thing, because practically everything on it is murder and crime and shooting and things of that kind. Where there are only adults in the home who are established in the faith, and have sense enough to turn off the trash of the world, and look only at that which is good, I don't suppose there is too much evil in it, but certainly where there are children in the home it is a damaging influence.

Chapter 8

CHURCH ORDINANCES

120. Are Christians Obligated to Take the Lord's Supper?

It is not necessary to go to church to observe the Lord's Table. Jesus said, "Where two or three are gathered in my Name, there am I in the midst." It is entirely Scriptural for two or more Christians to come together anywhere to remember the Lord.

However, according to Hebrews 10:25, we should assemble with God's people whenever possible.

121. What Do You Believe Concerning Feet Washing?

A careful study of the 13th chapter of John will reveal that the entire procedure of the Lord Jesus Christ was a local practice designed to teach His disciples not to wash one another's feet, but the deeper significance of true servitude and ministering one to another. The fact that it is not recorded to have been practiced by the apostles is only added proof that the scriptural lesson is the one which is the important thing, and not merely the physical ordinance. Jesus said in John 6:63, "It is the spirit that quickeneth; the flesh profiteth nothing; the words that I speak unto you, they are spirit, and they are life."

122. What Is the Meaning of "Eating Flesh and Drinking Blood?"

In regard to your question concerning eating flesh and drinking blood of the Lord Jesus Christ, I think that John

6:60-63 will explain your problem. In verse 63 Jesus says, "It is the Spirit that quickeneth; the flesh profiteth nothing." The eating of the flesh and drinking of the blood of Christ refers to the spiritual appropriation of all the benefits of His life and death on the Cross for us.

123. Should Only Unleavened Bread Be Used for the Lord's Supper, or Can Ordinary Bread Be Used?

Fellowship is of more importance than the kind of bread, and so where it is impossible to use the kind of bread that you feel should be used, there is no reason why you should not overlook this difference and fellowship with them anyway. If you will read carefully John 6:63, you will see that the spiritual significance is more important than the material elements. The Lord, I believe, understands these difficulties and makes allowances for them.

124. Do You Believe That the Communion Service Should Be Closed to Just the Members of the Church?

I personally do not believe that the Lord's Table is the table of any particular church or denomination. I believe that all born-again Christians who are not under Scriptural discipline should be invited to fellowship at the Lord's Table. If the believer is not living a life of separation, it is the duty of the assembly to deal with him, but apart from this the Bible says, "let a man examine himself." Anyone whom the Lord admits to the table should certainly be admitted by us. Closed communion is a pharisaical evidence of legalism and self-righteousness.

125. Who Are the Scriptural Officers of the Church, and What Is the Duty of Their Office?

In regard to bishops, deacons, elders and stewards, the three are mentioned in Scripture, while stewards are not mentioned as officers in the church.

An elder means simply, "an aged one," and is referred to both men and women. Paul speaks of the elder women and uses the same word. An elder is simply a person in the church who because of years of faithful service is recognized as a leader.

A bishop is an elder who is officially appointed to the office of teaching, preaching, advising and serving.

"Deacon" comes from a word which means "errand boy," and is one who is to take care of the poor. Deacons in Scripture are never given authority to rule or govern, but are merely to serve in this way.

As to stewards, we are all stewards.

126. Do You Believe That the Punishment of Taking the Lord's Supper Unworthily Is Literal Physical Sickness and Death?

In regard to your question concerning the Lord's Supper, I agree with you that few Christians live as close to the Lord as they should, but remember that the Lord is long-suffering and kind, and does not always immediately visit His children, but bears with them in great patience. There is no question that I Corinthians 11, however, speaks of physical sickness, weakness and death. This is in harmony with the rest of Scripture.

127. Must Ministers Be Ordained by the Church to Preach?

There is nothing in the entire Bible that individuals should be ordained by any denomination or any organization whatsoever. Men are ordained by God, chosen by God, fitted by God and sent forth to proclaim His message. Whether anyone has a "Reverend" or a "D.D." makes no difference whatsoever. This is merely a Catholic tradition.

128. Should Fasting and Prayer Be Observed by the Church in This Dispensation?

Fasting seems to have been more of a Jewish custom and it disappeared as the Church became more fully Gentile. I do not see any harm in fasting, although I do not believe that it is a commandment for this present age. I believe that the matter of fasting is one of personal opinion. If the Lord lays it upon one's heart to fast and pray, I am sure that no one can find fault with that. There are a great many different opinions on this matter. We believe that in general, fasting is not for this dispensation, but when we say this we want to make it clear that if the Lord by His spirit moves upon anyone's heart to set aside periods of fasting and prayer in order to be in an attitude of repentance so that God's blessing may come upon us, it is a matter of individual privilege and responsibility. I do not believe the Lord wants us to fast to the extent of injuring our health.

129. Is the Ordinance of the Lord's Supper for This Dispensation?

In regard to your question concerning the Lord's Supper, I am quite familiar with the teaching that the Lord's Supper does not belong in this dispensation. It certainly cannot be a Jewish ordinance when the Lord said, "Do this in remembrance of Me." The Church, the body of Christ, is to remember the price that Jesus paid and it is to be observed till He comes again. The command to the Corinthians was made to Christian Corinthians. The Jews had the Passover before the Cross, and the church has the Lord's Supper after the Cross.

130. Should Wine or Grape Juice Be Used at the Lord's Table?

In answering this question, it is significant that the Lord Jesus Christ and the apostles never used the word "wine" when referring to the Lord's Table. Instead they used the words, "fruit of the vine" or "cup." Since the word, "wine," is never used, we can infer that it need not necessarily be wine. However, let everyone be persuaded in his own mind.

131. I Have Had Trouble with a Man In My Church, and Am Wondering If I Can Scripturally Partake of the Lord's Supper at This Time.

There is only one thing you can do. If you have wronged this man you speak of, you should go to him and confess your wrong. If he has wronged you, it is not your responsibility. If you are right with the Lord and have made an effort to get the trouble out of the way, nothing should keep you from partaking of the Lord's Supper. Remember, however, to follow the instructions of Jesus in Matthew 18:15-17.

132. Can I Take the Lord's Supper Alone?

If there are two or more believers in your family, it is perfectly all right to remember the Lord in your home. Jesus said, "Where two or three are gathered together in my Name, there am I in the midst." If there are other believers in the community, it might be well to gather with them and fellowship around the table of the Lord. Where there is no assembly or other fellowship, it is perfectly all right to break bread with your own loved ones in your home. In Bible times they went from house to house breaking bread.

133. Must I Be Baptized Before I Can Partake of the Lord's Supper?

I believe that baptism is a testimony of salvation, and not a requisite of salvation. The only requirement for salvation and fellowship is faith in the Lord Jesus Christ. Since the Lord's Supper is a place for fellowship, the only requirement for partaking is salvation through faith. Baptism is not a requirement for partaking of the Lord's Supper.

134. I Am an Invalid and Unable to Get Out. Do You Think It Would Be Advisable for My Mother and Me to Partake of the Lord's Supper in the Privacy of Our Home; and If So, Please Give Us Some Instructions in Regard to How Often We Should Do It, and What Procedure We Should Follow?

The Lord Jesus Himself said, "Where two or three are gathered together in my Name, there am I in the midst." The simplest form of a Church, therefore, is where two or three believers come together in the Name of the Lord Jesus Christ. Such, of course, are allowed to remember the Lord's death in the Lord's Supper. You and your mother together can do this acceptably to the Lord by reading the appropriate passages of Scripture, such as I Corinthians 11, and also the passages of Scripture concerning the Lord's passion and death in the gospels and His institution of the Lord's Supper.

As a rule we use grape juice and bread for this matter. There is no reason why you, your mother and any other born-again believers cannot come together on the first day of the week, break bread, engage in prayer, remembering the Lord in this way. There is nothing in the Bible to indicate that only preachers can administer the Lord's Supper. It seems to have been the custom in the early church for the disciples to break bread every Lord's Day.

135. What Is the Significance of Circumcision?

The primary meaning of circumcision is a national sign to the nation of Israel to identify them as a peculiar people of God, distinguishing them and separating them from the Gentiles.

Spiritual circumcision represents the cutting away of the filth of the flesh and speaks of Christian separation from the world unto God.

CHAPTER 9

CHURCHES, ISMS AND RELIGIONS

136. What Is the Meaning of the Word, "Catholic"?

The word "catholic" means "universal," and really does not apply to the Roman Catholic religion any more than it does to us. They have monopolized the name and it is better to use the word, "universal," than "catholic."

137. Do You Think That a Fundamental Church Should Join the Federal Council of Churches?

The Federal Council of Churches has in its membership modernists of the worst type who deny many of the fundamentals for which we stand, such as the virgin birth of Christ, His deity, the blood atonement and the second coming of the Lord. Working with them would be endorsing a program in which any true, born-again Christian should not have a part.

138. What Is the National Council of Churches?

This is something on the same order as the Federal Council. I am afraid of some of these new organizations which do not go all the way in acknowledging the deity of the Lord Jesus Christ and other fundamental principles.

139. We Have Moved to a New Community and Wonder Where We Should Go to Church. Can You Help Us?

It is impossible to recommend to you a single denomination, since the local congregation depends so much upon the local pastor. I would suggest that you go to a good

76

fundamental church where the truth of the death, resurrection and second coming of the Lord Jesus Christ is plainly taught. There are many false doctrines being taught today and one must be exceedingly careful about where one goes for spiritual food.

140. Which Church Do You Consider the Best?

It would be quite impossible for me to advise you which church is the best. I am a Baptist because I believe it is nearest the Scriptural example. However, people of different nationality and different temperament sometimes react differently to various forms of worship.

The Episcopal Church, is the ultraritualistic, while the Plymouth Brethren are on the other extreme of simplicity. I believe that wherever the true gospel of Christ is preached one can find fellowship and worship. Denominations are man-made, you know, and there have been Godly men in all denominations. After all, there is only one True Church, the Body of Christ, consisting of all born-again believers, no matter to what denomination they may belong. The most important question is, "Am I a member of the Body of Christ?"

141. The Church of Which I Am a Member Has Become Modernistic, and I Am Concerned As to Just What I Ought to Do. Can You Please Help Me in This Problem?

In regard to the problem concerning your affiliation with a church which is connected with the Federal Council of Churches, I can deeply appreciate your position and the dilemma in which you find yourself. Our early associations are precious to us and it is not easy to break both with the church and with friends which we have had for so many years. Therefore, 1 would advise you not to be in too much of a hurry, but to seek the will of the Lord, and if you keep on praying and working, I believe that He will make His way clear to you. There are still many churches which have not affiliated themselves with modernism. I do not know about the conditions in your city, but if you will inquire and look around you will find a fellowship where you will not have to violate your conscience in regard to your affiliation with a movement which is definitely modernistic.

142. Who Are the Mormons and What Do They Teach?

The Mormons, or Latter Day Saints, are followers of the religion of Joseph Smith, a false cult which originated during the last century and is based not upon the Bible, but upon certain spurious gold plates which Joseph Smith claimed he found in the East years ago, containing the revelation of God.

143. I Have Become Connected with the Movement Called "Unity." What Do You Think of Their Doctrine?

Have nothing whatsoever to do with them. Unity is a false cult which denies the fundamental truths of the Bible. It does not teach the blood and plan of salvation as it is given by the Lord Jesus Christ. I believe it to be a dangerous error and would suggest that you break with it just as soon as possible.

144. I Have Become Confused by the Teachings of the Seventh Day Adventists Concerning the Keeping of the Sabbath. Can You Help Me?

I am indeed sorry that you have been confused by the teachings of the Seventh Day Adventists. It is absolutely true that the sabbath has never been changed, but you must remember that the Christian is not under the law, but under grace. If we are under grace, and not under the law, then naturally the sabbath does not apply to us any more. The seventh day, Saturday, is still the Jewish sabbath, but if you are not a Jew, you have no right to pay any attention to it. The Lord's Day, the first day of the week, is the Christian's day of fellowship and service. The whole thing depends upon whether you are under the law or under grace. If you are under the law, then you are not saved. If you are under grace (Ephesians 2:8), then you are saved. I think this will settle the question for you when you think it through. The sabbath is part of the law. You, if you have trusted the Lord Jesus Christ, are under grace, and therefore, are not obligated to keep the sabbath in any way.

The Seventh Day Adventists with their unscriptural teaching are doing a great deal of damage to God's dear people by placing them under the law. Remember that Christ is the fulfillment of the law for you. His work is finished and all you need to do is to trust Him.

145. What Do You Think of the Roman Catholic Church?

As a rule I make it a policy not to attack another denomination, but to preach the Gospel of Jesus Christ. There are many dear people in the Catholic Church, although we do not believe the organization itself is Scriptural. The Catholic Church as a whole is in darkness concerning God's simple plan of salvation. However, we pray for the people in it that they may have their eyes opened to the truth of God, and know that when they see the glorious grace of God, they cannot be satisfied any more with the religion of works. God Himself will deal with this apostate religion. (See Revelation 17 and 18.)

146. Which Church Is the True Church?

Concerning the one true Church, Scripture is explicit. In Ephesians, chapter 2, beginning at verse 19, we have the constitution of the Church as consisting of all true saints. In Ephesians 4 we are told there is one body, and

in Ephesians 3 we are told that this body consists of Jews
and Gentiles.

In Matthew 16, Christ establishes the one true Church
upon the confession that Peter made of Jesus as the Son
of God, and in Matthew 18, we have the conduct in
this Church described, in verses 15 to 20. There is one
Church consisting of the Body of Christ, constituted of all
members, black, white, Catholic, Protestant, Jew or Gentile,
who have trusted the finished work of Christ.

147. Who Are the "Jehovah's Witnesses," and Are Their Teachings According to the Scriptures?

It is hard to keep track of this sect, since they have
changed their name a great many times since they were first
inaugurated through the teachings of Pastor Russell.
They once were called "Russellites"; then they became the
"International Bible Students." Later on they changed their
name to "Millennial Dawnists," and their most recent name
is "Jehovah's Witnesses." They are zealous for their particular view, but since they deny the eternal existence of
the Lord Jesus Christ, the efficacy of the blood and the
atonement, I feel that they are one of the evils of these
latter days which the Lord warned us against when He
told us not to be deceived by the many false teachers. I
feel that while many of the members of the Jehovah's
Witness cult are sincere and earnest in their belief, that
they are wrong as far as the fundamentals of the Word of
God are concerned. We should be much in prayer that
we may be charitable toward those who disagree with us,
and at the same time, that we may be protected from the er-
rors which we know will be characteristic of the closing
days of this dispensation. While we disagree with them, we
should continue to pray for them.

148. Must I Join a Church to Be a Good Christian?

If we are believers, we will seek the fellowship of other Christians round about us. If there is a church in your community that preaches the gospel of the Lord Jesus Christ in all its fulness, where you can have sweet fellowship, it is your duty to affiliate yourself and to enter into the activities of this church. When there is no church in your community where the Gospel is truly preached, you are better off not giving your endorsement to a movement which is not of the Lord. Remember that there is no perfect church as far as the local organization is concerned here upon the earth, and we must overlook the imperfections in the people and in the leaders, realizing that we ourselves are still quite imperfect also. I do not know just what the situation is in your community, so I would advise you to fellowship with God's people as long as they are true to the Word. If this is impossible, it is better for you to limit yourself to the radio, and seek as many Christian friends as you possibly can in your immediate community.

149. What Is Your Opinion of the Christian Science Religion?

Christian Science is a clever delusion, which is neither "Christian" nor "scientific." Christian Science denies the blood of the Lord Jesus Christ, the new birth, but is the teaching of a woman by the name of Mrs. Eddy and not the Word of God.

150. Is "Spiritism" a Christian Religion?

In I Timothy 4:1 and I John 4:1-3 we are very definitely told that in the latter days demon activity will be prevalent and that it will be a sign of apostasy by which multitudes will be deceived. Spiritism denies all the fundamentals of the Christian faith.

151. What Is Your Opinion of the Writings of Emanuel Swedenborg?

I have studied his philosophy and feel that he was in error. I do not for one moment doubt his sincerity, but many of his teachings are directly opposed to the clear revelation of the Word of God. He was undoubtedly a deep thinker, a bright scholar and a sincere student, but came to erroneous and wrong conclusions.

152. Do You Recommend Reading the Works of E. Stanley Jones?

E. Stanley Jones is considered by many fundamentalists as leaning very strongly to the modernistic side of theology.

153. Can You Give Me Some Information Concerning the Teachings of Bullingerism?

There is a great deal of agitation concerning the revival of the doctrine of Bullingerism in these last days, and I have investigated it from every angle. We have three different groups of "Drys." First, we have those who do not believe in baptism, but still observe the Lord's Supper. A second group has thrown out both baptism and the Lord's Supper, which is quite consistent. If we throw out one, both should go. And then we have a third group who have gone all the way, and not only reject the ordinances, but eternal punishment, and teach final restitution and soul sleeping.

We believe all these extremes of ultra-dispensationalism to be a delusion and perversion of the truth.

CHAPTER 10

CHURCHES: THEIR SUPPORT AND PROGRAM

154. Do You Think There Will Be a Revival Before the Lord Returns?

I do not know whether there will be a revival before the Lord comes. If the Lord tarries, we do need a great awakening, and I do believe that God is more than ready to send us a revival if we as God's people are able to make ourselves willing to receive it. Let us continue to pray that if the Lord tarries, there will be a great revival among God's people.

The entire content of Scripture tells us that this age will end in violence and apostasy. While there will continue to be local revivals and refreshings, we do not believe that this age will end in a world-wide revival. If we are wrong, and it does come, we are going to give God the glory just the same.

155. Is It Necessary for a Christian to Attend Church?

We believe that it is the duty of Christians to assemble themselves together (Hebrews 10:25) on the Lord's Day with God's people whenever it is possible to meet with those who preach the whole Bible in purity. However, where it is impossible to receive the proper spiritual food in your own church, it is better to remain at home and get your soul fed through good fundamental gospel programs than to be starved by modernistic preaching.

156. Should the Tithe Be One-Tenth?

In regard to tithing, one-tenth was given as commanded in the law in Malachi. Under grace we certainly should not give less than under the law, so that today the tithe plus an offering is still the least that a Christian should give to the work of the Lord.

157. Is Tithing Required for This Dispensation?

Many believe that tithing is an Old Testament institution, but when you recall Abraham gave tithes to Melchizedek and Jacob gave tithes to the Lord long before the age of law, you will see that it applies to the age of grace as well. The tithe was the minimum by the law and cannot be any less than that under grace. It is a fact that they who set a tenth aside for the Lord are unusually blessed by the Lord.

158. Must All Our Tithe Be Placed in the Local Church?

There is no Scripture which tells people that their tithes have to go into any particular local organization. The storehouse in Israel as we have it in Malachi was the place where all gifts were brought for the entire religious life of the nation and for the temple worship. All the needs of all God's work were supplied out of the storehouse. We personally believe that if preachers would be more unselfish that their own personal needs would be much more abundantly supplied. We are one body and have one interest. While the local church needs support, we believe that God has raised up the radio ministry to reach countless thousands that cannot and will not be touched by the church. This work must, of course, be supported by those who love the Lord.

159. Does the Bible Say Anything Against Having Socials in the Church?

In I Corinthians 11:22-34 Paul's words are clear that we have houses to eat and to drink in. The danger is that these social events become the big things in the church, while the spiritual angle is neglected.

160. What Do You Think of Having Church Sales and Suppers?

The 11th chapter of I Corinthians is definite in teaching that the assembly of God's people is for the purpose of fellowship, teaching and breaking of bread. If you will read the chapter carefully, you will notice that the evil of eating and banqueting in the church is strictly forbidden. In the entire book of Acts we find no reference in the early church of suppers, sales, banqueting, entertaining, or other foolishness. The business of the Lord is too serious to mix with worldly things.

161. Do You Think It Is All Right to Use Moving Pictures in the Church?

It is rather difficult to give a satisfactory answer in view of conditions today. The service should be one of preaching and not showing of pictures. "Faith cometh by hearing," and not by seeing. It seems to me that the tendency to bring in pictures, both still and moving, is an admission on our part that our preaching is not powerful enough to get people to listen, and so we have to adopt worldly methods in order to make up for it. I realize that in many good fundamental churches pictures are shown, but if I could have my way, I certainly would rather not have them, but stick to the old-fashioned preaching service. If pictures are to be shown, it would be better to set aside a weekday in some place beside the church.

162. I Have Had a Discussion with a Friend Who Attends A Church Where Music on Instruments Is Not Permitted. Is This According to Scripture?

Both in the Old Testament and in the New Testament there is sufficient evidence that music was used in the worship of the people. There is no record of instruments ever being used in the New Testament. However, at the same time there is abundant mention made of musical instruments in the Old Testament worship. Personally, I have no objections to instrumental music if it is used to the glory of God. However, if a group of Christians today do not believe in instrumental music, and can agree among themselves to use human voices, that is their privilege and liberty.

163. The Church Which I Attend Is Giving a Series of Programs Dramatizing Certain Records of the Bible. I Am Not in Accord with This, and Wonder If You Could Be of Help to Me in this Matter.

There are various shades of opinion in regard to this matter, and I am wholly in accord with you that the church is hardly the place for activities of this kind. The business of the church is that of fellowshipping around the Word of God, and preparing to go out and win precious souls for the Lord Jesus Christ. There is a tendency in these days to bring everything into the church, so that much of it, while it has a Biblical background, is largely for entertainment and appeals to the eye, rather than to the ear. In a matter of that kind, I can simply withdraw myself personally, and leave it up to the conscience of others to tell them what is right, and what is wrong. I believe this is the Biblical way to approach the situation. If you feel that it is not right for you to take part, then it would be wrong for you to do so. I advise you to follow the leading of the Spirit of the Lord as He shows you.

164. What Is Your Stand on the Matter of Having Recreational Activities in the Church?

Each church has to decide these things for themselves. I do not endorse these various recreational activities, especially not if they become a part of the program of the church. If our young people want to play baseball and have their different teams, etc., outside of the church under Christian supervision of some good friends, I have no objections, but the work of the church is to preach the Gospel of the Lord Jesus Christ, and to send out the glad message of salvation. Since there is already such a need for funds to send out the Gospel through missionary work and radio broadcasting as well as local church work, money expended by Christians through the church for recreational activities might better be placed somewhere else. If people want to personally, individually, give toward these things, it is their own business, but I do not think it should go through the church.

CHAPTER 11

DISCREPANCIES IN SCRIPTURE PASSAGES

In this chapter, rather than quote the questions as they
came in the mail relative to the Scripture passages, we
have arranged the passages in Bibliological order, since
most of the questions were inquiries concerning the interpretation of these various passages.

This material is in no way intended to be a commentary
or exposition, but rather a brief interpretation and outline
to aid in further study on any of these particular verses.
Questions concerning these passages have been asked over
and over again by many of our listeners. Since so many
have been especially puzzled by these particular Scripture
quotations, we trust that this brief outline study will also
aid you in "rightly dividing the Word of Truth."

165. Genesis 1 — Heaven

Concerning the creation story in Genesis 1, we must remember that in the Bible there are at least three different
words for "heaven." The first is "ouranos" which means
"the lower heavens," or the cloud heavens. Then there is
the word, "mesouranos," which means "middle heaven,"
or the planetary or astronomical heavens, and then there is
the word, "epouranos," which means the "upper heavens,"
or the super-heaven which is the "heaven of heavens."
What Genesis 1 is dealing with is the lower heaven of the
atmosphere, the clouds, the separation of the waters on the
earth, and above the earth. The firmament undoubtedly

means the separation of the waters in the atmosphere and the waters which are condensed on the earth. Then there is a second separation of the waters on the earth in one place, as distinguished from dry land.

166. Genesis 1:26 — The Trinity

And God said, Let us make man in our image, after our likeness.

This is just one of the many references in Scripture indicating that God is a trinity. The "let us," therefore, refers to the work of the Father, Son and Holy Spirit in creation.

167. Genesis 3:15 — The Protevangelium

And I will put enmity between thee and the woman, and between thy seed and her seed; it shall bruise thy head, and thou shalt bruise his heel.

I personally believe that in this promise there are two parts; one, the bruising of the heel of the seed of the woman, which, refers to Calvary; and the bruising of the head of the serpent, which refers to the ultimate victory of the Lord Jesus Christ over Satan. I base my opinion upon Romans 16:20 where we read: "And the God of peace shall bruise Satan under your feet shortly." Since Romans 16 was written about thirty years after the Cross of Calvary this is still future, so we infer from this passage that the bruising of the head of Satan refers to the ultimate victory of the Lord Jesus Christ when He comes again. I quite agree with you that it is our business to assist in every way possible to crush the head of Satan in these days of great wickedness and immorality.

168. Genesis 9:20-29 — The Curse of Noah

And Noah began to be an husbandman, and he planted a vineyard:

And he drank of the wine, and was drunken; and he was uncovered within his tent.

And Ham, the father of Canaan, saw the nakedness of his father, and told his two brethren without.

And Shem and Japheth took a garment, and laid it upon both their shoulders, and went backward, and covered the nakedness of their father; and their faces were backward, and they saw not their father's nakedness.

And Noah awoke from his wine, and knew what his younger son had done unto him.

And he said, Cursed be Canaan; a servant of servants shall he be unto his brethren.

And he said, Blessed be the Lord God of Shem; and Canaan shall be his servant.

God shall enlarge Japheth, and he shall dwell in the tents of Shem; and Canaan shall be his servant.

And Noah lived after the flood three hundred and fifty years.

And all the days of Noah were nine hundred and fifty years: and he died.

There is little doubt that the curse which Noah pronounced upon Canaan after his drunkenness was also the curse of God upon the descendants of Noah through his grandson. Of course, we must remember that colored people are not the only ones who are the descendants of Canaan. The Canaanites who were in the land of Palestine during the time of Abraham and since then, were also of the same stock, and these were also under the curse of Almighty God. I do not believe, however, that the black skin of the Negro is the result of this curse, but rather that this is the normal reaction toward the climatic conditions in which they have lived for many, many centuries. The constant exposure to the sun has caused their skin to become dark. There is no other physical difference between the colored people and the white races, except in the coloration of the skin and the outward characteristics of their features, in their hair and lips, etc. To use the curse

of Noah upon his descendants as an excuse for national prejudice and subjecting them to servitude is not Scriptural. The Bible has definitely stated that these descendants of Canaan would be the servants of the other nations of the world. This has been abundantly borne out throughout history in the fact that these nations have always been in a position of service and oftentimes in slavery. Instead of oppressing those who are under this peculiar curse, we ought to do everything in our power to make their way easier, and to remember that Christ died for them as well as for others, and seek to bring them the Gospel of our blessed Lord and Saviour Jesus Christ.

169. Genesis, chapter 27: — Jacob and Esau

In regard to your question concerning Esau and Jacob, you must remember that in verse 29 the Lord promises dominion to Jacob, but the actual carrying out of it would not come until later. Not only was Jacob afraid of Esau, and fled from him, but Israel suffered much from the descendants of Esau.

170. Genesis 49:10 — British Israelism

> The sceptre shall not depart from Judah, nor a lawgiver from between his feet, until Shiloh come; and unto him shall the gathering of the people be.

This verse is used by the British Israelites, but I do not believe that it gives them any reason whatsoever to suppose that the British nations are the lost ten tribes. This is part of Jacob's blessing upon his son, giving the promise that as long as Israel as a nation remains, the promise of the coming Redeemer and the coming Saviour, the Lord Jesus Christ, will never be abrogated. I believe that the 10th verse looks into the future when the Lord Jesus Christ shall sit upon the throne of David, and shall restore Israel in completeness and in fulness.

171. Exodus 34:28 and Deuteronomy 10:4 Who Wrote the Tables of the Law?

> And he was there with the Lord forty days and forty nights; he did neither eat bread, nor drink water. And he wrote upon the tables the words of the covenant, the ten commandments (Exodus 34:28).

> And he wrote on the tables, according to the first writing, the ten commandments, which the Lord spake unto you in the mount out of the midst of the fire in the day of the assembly: and the Lord gave them unto me (Deut. 10:4).

There was a three-fold giving of the "law." The first was given "orally" to Moses (Exodus 20:1-17). The second was written by the finger of God, and these tables were broken at the foot of the Mount by Moses (Exodus 31:18; 32:15-19). Then thirdly, the second tables were made by Moses and the "law" written upon it by the hand of God (Exodus 34:1, 28, 29; Deut. 10:4).

172. Leviticus 15:19-29 — Birth Control

Leviticus 15:19-29 is not in any sense a prevention of conception, but rather a control of conception. I believe that if this injunction is followed, that God will determine how close the children will be spaced. It is very well possible that when one faithfully follows the law of separation, the children may still come very closely. Then we have the assurance and the confidence that it was God who ordered it that way. The testimonies of multitudes of God's people is that it does work in the spacing of children according to the will of God.

173. II Samuel 12:13 and II Samuel 22:21-23 — The Two Natures

How are these Two Verses Reconciled?

> And David said unto Nathan, I have sinned against the Lord. And Nathan said unto David, The Lord also hath put away thy sin; thou shalt not die (II Sam. 12:13).

> The Lord rewarded me according to my righteousness:

according to the cleanness of my hands hath he recompensed me.

For I have kept the ways of the Lord, and have not wickedly departed from my God.

For all his judgments were before me: and as for his statutes, I did not depart from them (II Sam. 22:21-23).

In II Samuel 12:13 we have David's sin which he committed in the flesh. However, in II Samuel 22, David is speaking there as a justified saint before God, who has been forgiven and all his sins have been washed away. We must distinguish between the position of the believer in Christ, and his state as he is still here upon the earth. The Christian as he is through faith is justified, perfect and complete in the Lord Jesus. At the same time, however, he is still in the world, and the flesh and the old man are constantly with him, and these cannot do any good thing. When we distinguish between these two, we can see that one can be a forgiven sinner and at the same time be a righteous saint in the sight of God. We have the same thing in I John 1:8-10, where we have John speaking of the old nature, while in I John 3:9 he is speaking of the new nature which cannot sin.

174. I Chronicles 21:2 — David's Sin in Numbering Israel

And David said to Joab and to the rulers of the people, Go, number Israel from Beer-sheba, even to Dan; and bring the number of them to me, that I may know it (I Chron. 21:2).

David's sin in numbering the people was that it was instigated by pride. It was not his desire merely to number the people for a census purpose, but in order that he might know how strong he was. It was an indication that he was depending upon the army, rather than upon the arm of the Lord. This was the thing which the Lord condemned, and for which the judgment came upon the nation.

175. II Chronicles 7:14 — Does God Answer All Prayer?

> If my people, which are called by my name, shall humble themselves, and pray, and seek my face, and turn from their wicked ways; then will I hear from heaven, and will forgive their sin, and will heal their land. (I Chron. 7:14).

I realize that this was given primarily to Israel by interpretation, but by application all Scripture is for us as well. All Scripture has one primary interpretation, but it has many secondary applications. If we remember this, then we can use all of the Bible for our admonition and instruction.

176. The Book of Job

The lesson of the book of Job is the lesson of the sufferings of the Christian, and God's dealing with the believer in an effort to draw him closer unto Himself, not only to close the mouth of Satan, but also to prove to the world that God's people need chastening, and through this chastening are drawn closer unto Him.

177. Job, chapter 1 — Where Did the Devil Meet God?

It was not on the earth, but somewhere in the heavenlies. When the Bible speaks about the heavens, it may mean one of three things; the atmospheric heavens, or the planetary heavens, or the heaven of heavens. The Bible does not tell us distinctly where this took place. That Satan does have access to God for the purpose of accusing the brethren is perfectly clear from the Scriptures. However, many of the details are not given to us now, but we shall know when we see Him face to face.

178. Job 37:7 — Finger Printing in the Bible

> He sealeth up the hand of every man; that all men may know his work (Job 37:7).

I do not believe that Job 37:7 refers to finger printing.

The verse is a figure of speech to indicate the limitations of every man's work, so that no man can do anything without the will of the Lord. This is quite evident from the next verse where the control of God over even the beasts of the field is clearly indicated. We should be careful and not try to read into the Scripture anything which is not there. Many Bible teachers and evangelists find things in the Bible which even the Lord did not place there.

179. Psalm 91 — Does God Protect Us from All Harm?

In regard to the 91st Psalm, it is well that we remember that the primary interpretation is to the Person of the Lord Jesus Christ. This is evident when we realize that the 12th verse is quoted even by Satan at the temptation experience in the wilderness.

In regard to the religious cults which allow individuals to be bitten by snakes, I do not believe that this is ever the will of God. It is mere presumption. The fact that some recover means nothing at all, since in my practice of medicine I have seen many cases of snake bite which recovered, some of them when they received no treatment for a long time. To place ourselves wilfully in a place of danger certainly cannot be pleasing unto the Lord.

180. Psalm 119 — The Divisions of This Psalm

The titles of each of the divisions of this Psalm correspond to the letters of the Hebrew alphabet, from Aleph to Tau. It is a long Psalm, and the writer under inspiration divided it into various verses corresponding to the letters of the Hebrew alphabet. As you probably know, the Psalm was written in poetic form, and each one of these divisions represents one stanza of the poem.

181. Psalm 137:9 — Is the Atomic Bomb Mentioned in Scripture?

> Happy shall he be, that taketh and dasheth thy little ones against the stones (Psalm 137:9).

In regard to your question concerning Psalm 137:9, we would refer you to Isaiah 13:16. The verse contains the same expression, and this is evidently referring to the atomic bomb in the judgment of the Lord during the tribulation, as seen in verses 13 and 14 of Isaiah 13. What "these little ones" refers to we may not know, but children also perished in the flood and children also perish in wars today, so this has reference to the same thing. See also II Peter chapter 3.

182. Proverbs 14:12 — Does Proverbs 14:12 Teach Salvation by Grace?

> There is a way which seemeth right unto a man, but the end thereof are the ways of death (Prov. 14:12).

The way which seemeth right unto a man and is the way of death is the way of the flesh. It refers to the teaching that a man can be saved by his own works of righteousness, rather than by the grace of God. Adam and Eve tried it when they made coverings of fig leaves, but failed. Cain tried it when he brought his sacrifice, the work of his own hands. We are to remember that we are saved by grace, and never by works. The way of life is the way of grace, through faith. The way of death is the way of works and the law.

183. Ecclesiastes — How Do You Reconcile the Book of Ecclesiastes With the Rest of Scripture?

Concerning the passages in Ecclesiastes, you must remember that Ecclesiastes was written by Solomon, describing the course of man "under the sun." He speaks here not of the spiritual man, but of the physical man, and tells us that there is nothing new which man has ever discovered.

All the inventions and discoveries of science are based upon the things which God has already placed in nature, so that he is only applying the laws and the materials which God has already created in making the things which we call new inventions. In this respect, there is "nothing new under the sun."

In regard to Ecclesiastes 3:19, you must remember again that Solomon is speaking here about man in his physical condition, and he speaks here of physical death, so that death passes upon all creation, not only human beings, but upon animals as well. It has nothing to do with salvation of the soul, but only with man's physical life.

184. Song of Solomon 8:5 — Who is the Bridegroom in Song of Solomon 8:5?

Who is this that cometh up from the wilderness, leaning upon her beloved?

In regard to your question concerning Song of Solomon, chapter 8 and verse 5. I am thoroughly convinced that this has reference to the Lord Jesus Christ as the Bridegroom of the Church. The entire Song of Solomon is a love story between the Bride and the Bridegroom.

185. Isaiah 4:1 — What Does It Mean That "Seven Women Shall Take Hold of One Man" in Isaiah 4?

The fourth chapter of Isaiah must be read in the light of the last part of the third chapter, where the Lord pronounces judgment on Israel and Judah because of their sin. As a result of God's judgment so many of the men of Israel will fall in battle that there will be seven women for each man that is left. It speaks of God's judgment on Israel in the day of Jacob's trouble.

186. Isaiah 28:20 — What Does Isaiah Refer to When Speaking of a "Short Bed" in Isaiah 28:20?

> For the bed is shorter than that a man can stretch himself on it: and the covering narrower than that he can wrap himself in it (Isaiah 28:20).

This is a figure of speech by which the prophet Isaiah is trying to impress the children of Israel with the hopelessness and the uselessness of seeking to save themselves by their own means. Instead of going to the Lord with all their troubles, they were going to the nations round about them, trying to solve their own problems in their own way. The Lord compares this effort on the part of the nation of Israel to a man who tries to keep warm in a bed which is too short for him, and where he has insufficient covering. It is an oriental figure of speech designed to bring the message to Israel of the imperative necessity of turning to the Lord for their only salvation.

187. Isaiah 31:5 — Does This Verse Refer to Airplanes?

> As birds flying, so will the Lord of hosts defend Jerusalem; defending also he will deliver it; and passing over he will preserve it (Isaiah 31:5).

It is agreed by a great many Bible students that this refers to the airplanes of the latter days. (See also Ezekiel 38:9 and 16.)

188. Isaiah 52:7 — Speaks of Beautiful Feet. Whose Are They?

> How beautiful upon the mountains are the feet of him that bringeth good tidings, that publisheth peace; that bringeth good tidings of good, that publisheth salvation; that saith unto Zion, Thy God reigneth! (Isaiah 52:7).

You will find the explanation of this in Romans 10:15. It refers to the ministry of those who have been commissioned of the Lord to bear the Gospel of good tidings to a lost world. It is a picture of one who runs with the message, and God calls their feet "beautiful upon the mountains" because they carry the good message of salvation.

189. Isaiah 63:3 — What Is Referred to As the "Winepress" in Isaiah 63:3?

I have trodden the winepress alone; and of the people there was none with me; for I will tread them in mine anger, and trample them in my fury; and their blood shall be sprinkled upon my garments, and I will stain all my raiment (Isaiah 63:3).

This speaks of the Lord Jesus Christ in His first and second coming. At Calvary He trod the winepress alone, and when He comes again, He will trample His enemies in His fury.

190. Jeremiah 10:2-5 — Does This Refer to the Christmas Tree?

Thus saith the Lord, Learn not the way of the heathen, and be not dismayed at the signs of heaven; for the heathen are dismayed at them.

For the customs of the people are vain: for one cutteth a tree out of the forest, the work of the hands of the workman, with the axe.

They deck it with silver and with gold; they fasten it with nails and with hammers, that it move not.

They are upright as the palm tree, but speak not (Jeremiah 10:2-5).

The context of this passage seems to indicate that the trees there were actually worshipped as idols. However, the similarity to our Christmas trees is so striking that it certainly is suggestive. Certainly Christmas trees are of pagan origin.

191. What Are the "Speckled Birds" in Jeremiah 12:8?

In regard to your question concerning the speckled bird, you will find the reference in Jeremiah 12:8 as follows:

Mine heritage is unto me as a speckled bird, the birds

round about are against her; come ye, assemble all the
beasts of the field, come to devour.

Now if you will read the context, you will notice that
the reference here is first of all to the nation of Israel who
in the providence of God are speckled birds, never to be
assimilated among the nations, but to be kept separate because of God's program for them, when they shall be
restored in the land of Palestine.

192. Does Ezekiel 13:18 Refer to Padded Clothing?

And say, thus saith the Lord God; Woe to the women that
sew pillows to all armholes, and make kerchiefs upon the
head of every stature to hunt souls! Will ye hunt the souls
of my people, and will ye save the souls alive that come
unto you? (Ezekiel 13:18)

It is well to remember that the prophet here is speaking
against and denouncing false prophets who were speaking
in the Name of the Lord in Israel, but had never been sent
by God Himself. Among these were some women who
claimed that they were prophets of the Lord, and were
speaking falsely to the children of Israel. The practice of
these women was to carry on their elbows a bag that looked
something like a pillow in which they carried their material
whereby they claimed to be sent of the Lord. These bags
were something like the phylacteries which the Jews later
carried upon their heads. The word, "pillow," here really
means a "sack" or a "bag," and was not worn upon the
shoulders, but according to the original Hebrew it was
usually swung from the elbow. It has nothing to do with
the padding of clothes as we see it today. In the next verse,
the "kerchief" is also a wrong translation. It means "veil"
and refers to the veil or special dress which these women
wore as they sought to prophesy. It was a peculiar
dress of those who called themselves the servants of the
Lord. These are the things which Ezekiel denounced.

193. Ezekiel 18:22 — Does Ezekiel 18:22 Teach That Men Can Be Saved by Being Good?

> All his transgressions that he hath committed, they shall not be mentioned unto him: in his righteousness that he hath done he shall live (Ezekiel 18:22).

You must remember in reading the prophecy of Ezekiel as well as the Old Testament prophets that they were speaking under the law before Calvary and before the full plan of grace for this dispensation was made known. While they were saved by faith, they were still under the law as a schoolmaster to bring them to Christ. The law said, "do this or die," but when Christ came He abolished the law (See I Corinthians 3), and brought in grace. John says the law came by Moses, but grace and truth came by Jesus Christ. Hence, to quote from Ezekiel except in the light of the New Testament grace is to get the wrong application entirely.

194. Ezekiel 34 — Who Are the False Shepherds in Ezekiel 34?

Concerning the shepherds spoken of in Ezekiel 34, these are not the Gentiles, but are the false teachers and priests of Israel who had led the people astray. If you will read the chapter carefully, you will notice that the context indicates that this is the proper interpretation. We believe that it has reference also to the false teachers in Israel today who are causing God's people to reject the Messiah, the Lord Jesus Christ, whereas He came to be their Saviour.

195. What Are the "Two Sticks" in Ezekiel 37?

In regard to Ezekiel 37, I think that if you will read the chapter carefully, you will find the explanation right there. In the 16th verse we are told that one stick represents the nation of Judah, and the other stick represents Ephraim, or the house of Israel. Judah represents the southern Kingdom of Israel after the division under Rehoboam, and Ephraim and Israel represent the Northern Ten Tribes. And in this chapter, the prophet is predicting that the time will come when both these two Kingdoms, in fact, the twelve tribes of Israel, shall be completely united and brought back again into the land. It is the same as the revival of the dry bones in the preceding verses in Ezekiel 37.

196. Ezekiel 38 and 39 — Is Modern Russia Mentioned in the Bible?

I am convinced that Ezekiel 38 and 39 refer to Russia and her satellites, who will be one of the main factors in the battle during the tribulation period. When Russia seeks to conquer the Holy Land, it will be the signal for the return of the Lord Jesus Christ in glory, and then He will defeat their armies and set up His Kingdom. A careful study of this chapter will bear this out, I think.

197. Will the Nations Use Bows and Arrows Again in the Latter Days?

Concerning Ezekiel 38 and 39, you must remember that God used the prophets in the time in which they lived, and bows and arrows being the instruments of war would mean the same as though we speak today of tanks and cannon and airplanes. The Lord in inspiring the prophets left them in the environment of the age in which they lived.

198. Do Ezekiel 38 and 39 Refer to the Communistic Nations?

Yes, there is no question that this refers to the Northern army and the confederacy which is now forming with Russia at its head. This army, of course, will swoop down, and in the contest over Palestine will temporarily be defeated by the Roman beast. Finally, at the end of the tribulation, all the armies of the world will be gathered at the

Battle of Armageddon, to be destroyed by the Lord Himself. While there are many things which are not clear, and there is much difference of opinion concerning some of these matters, we can only state these things as we see them, without being dogmatic, and await the time when we shall see the complete fulfillment of all the Word of the Lord.

199. Ezekiel 43:19-27 — Will the Old Testament Sacrifices be Restored in the Millennium?

The feasts, according to Ezekiel, will be kept during the millennium as a memorial of the death of Christ, rather than a prophetic picture of the death of Christ, as we today commemorate the death of the Lord Jesus Christ in the Lord's Supper.

200. What Is Meant By the "Daily Sacrifice" In Daniel 12:11?

And from the time that the daily sacrifice shall be taken away, and the abomination that maketh desolate set up, there shall be a thousand two hundred and ninety days (Daniel 12:11).

The daily sacrifice found in the 12th chapter of Daniel is the offering which was brought each day by the priest according to Leviticus. This will be restored and then caused to cease by the antichrist during the tribulation period.

201. Please Explain Amos 5:18-20.

Woe unto you that desire the day of the Lord! to what end is it for you? the day of the Lord is darkness, and not light.

As if a man did flee from a lion, and a bear met him; or went into the house, and leaned his hand on the wall, and a serpent bit him.

Shall not the day of the Lord be darkness, and not light? even very dark, and no brightness in it? (Amos 5:18-20).

In regard to your question concerning Amos 5:18-20, we must remember that the Lord here is speaking with individuals who were not serving Him. In the 21st verse we read how God despised their hypocritical feast days, and their empty religious worship. To all such, the coming of the Lord is a day of doom and blackness and darkness, and not the Blessed Hope which it is for believers who will be taken out before the tribulation period. These people were imagining that they were all right, and that when the Lord came it would be for their blessing. And the Lord reminds them that when He comes, and those who are left behind will have to go through the day of the Lord, it will be a terrible experience. The entire chapter is one of judgment upon a nation that had forsaken the Lord their God. Of course, we realize that in this nation there still was a remnant, who were looking for the hope of Israel and serving the Lord in sincerity, just as today there are many who have religion but never have been born again, but we do thank God for that remnant who are faithful to His promise.

202. Jonah 2 — Did Jonah Die in the Belly of the Whale?

If you will read the second chapter of Jonah carefully, you will notice that in verse 1, Jonah prayed to God from "the belly of the whale," but in verse 2, he prayed to God from "the belly of hell." The word translated "hell" here is the Hebrew word, "sheol," which occurs many times in the Bible, and in every single instance always means "the abode of the dead," or the place where the dead go. It is the same place to which Jesus is said to go in Psalm 16 and Acts 2. From these passages we must believe that Jonah was in sheol, and since sheol is the place of the dead, Jonah of necessity must have been dead. Furthermore, Jonah tells us in verse 7 that the Lord had brought him up from corruption. It does not say that the Lord had spared him from corruption, but had "brought him up from corruption." From these and other evidences, it is quite clear that Jonah as a perfect type of the Lord Jesus Christ in His death, burial and resurrection, actually died in the fish, and the miracle of Jonah consists in the fact that God raised him from the dead as a perfect type of the Gospel of our crucified, buried and risen Lord.

203. Who Are the Two Olive Trees in Zechariah 4:3 and the Two Witnesses in Revelation 11:4?

And two olive trees by it, one upon the right side of the bowl, and the other upon the left side thereof (Zech. 4:3).

These are the two olive trees, and the two candlesticks standing before the God of the earth (Rev. 11:4).

The olive trees in these two passages are the same. They represent the two witnesses during the tribulation period after the rapture of the Church. I believe that these two witnesses will be Moses and Elijah who will prophesy for a period of three and one-half years, be put to death, then raised again. It will be through their testimony largely that the 144,000 Jews will be converted during the tribulation period.

204. What Is Meant by the "Long Day" in Zechariah 14?

The passage in Zechariah 14 is a direct reference to the Day of the Lord, and more particularly to the Battle of Armageddon. The Lord will lengthen that day as He did in the time of Joshua, in order to give sufficient time and opportunity for the accomplishment of His purpose in judging the nations and the nation of Israel. Immediately after this, the millennium will be inaugurated.

205. What Is the Meaning of the Fourteen Generations in Matthew 1:17?

So all the generations from Abraham to David are fourteen generations; and from David until the carrying away into Babylon are fourteen generations; and from the carrying away into Babylon unto Christ are fourteen generations (Matt. 1:17).

In regard to your question, evidently the fourteen generations mentioned three times in Matthew 1:17 refers to the numerical dealings of God with Israel in periods of 490 years. Fourteen is twice the perfect number, and since it is mentioned three times, it speaks to us of God's faithfulness in His covenant dealings with Abraham, David and Israel.

206. Why Are We Told to Agree with Our Adversaries in Matthew 5:25-26?

Agree with thine adversary quickly, whiles thou art in the way with him; lest at any time the adversary deliver thee to the judge, and the judge deliver thee to the officer, and thou be cast into prison.

Verily I say unto thee, Thou shalt by no means come out thence, till thou hast paid the uttermost farthing (Matt. 5:25-26).

The entire meaning of this is that we are not to seek or to make trouble, but rather agree with those who oppose us, if it is at all possible, lest we suffer for our own rebellion. This has a very wide application, and it is impossible to say just exactly who the adversary or the officer or the judge might be.

Just remember, Jesus is speaking in this passage concerning our conduct in the world toward our fellow man, and particularly the brethren. He tells us here we are to make every effort to remain at peace, to be willing to be the least for the sake of avoiding strife. I am sure that if this principle were practiced in the world today, there would be no war. We are even told to make friends of the mammon of unrighteousness (Luke 16:9).

207. Why Are We Told to Pluck Out Our Eyes in Matthew 5:29?

And if thy right eye offend thee, pluck it out, and cast it from thee: for it is profitable for thee that one of thy members should perish, and not that thy whole body should be cast into hell (Matt. 5:29).

In Matthew 5:29-30, there are two things which you must remember. One is that this is part of the Sermon on the Mount, and has to do with the Kingdom message of the Lord Jesus Christ. While all of this is true, it is still also true that we are to take this literally. It is literally much better for a man to lose his eye or to lose a hand or a foot, than to be lost forever in hell. No physical loss of any of our members can compare to the loss of a man's soul eternally in the place of condemnation.

208. Please Explain the Meaning of "Casting Pearls Before Swine" in Matthew 7:6.

Give not that which is holy unto the dogs, neither cast ye your pearls before swine, lest they trample them under their feet, and turn again and rend you (Matt. 7:6).

Now in regard to Matthew 7:6, you must remember that the Lord Jesus Christ was talking to unbelieving Pharisees. He had been speaking to them and admonishing them, but they had turned their backs upon all of His teaching. And now the time has come when the Lord Jesus does not feel justified anymore in wasting time on those who will not hear and will not believe.

The application for us is simply this. There are times when we have done our best to witness to men and women, and we are not obligated to do so any more. Often we meet people who when we talk to them about the Lord Jesus Christ, only jeer and laugh, and sometimes it even makes them worse. I believe that there comes a time when we are not expected to work on them anymore, but use our testimony in more productive channels.

209. Who Are the Children of the Kingdom to Be Cast into Outer Darkness Mentioned in Matthew 8:12 and Matthew 22:13?

> But the children of the kingdom shall be cast out into outer darkness: there shall be weeping and gnashing of teeth (Matt. 8:12).
>
> Then said the king to the servants, Bind him hand and foot, and take him away, and cast him into outer darkness; there shall be weeping and gnashing of teeth (Matt. 22:13).

In regard to your question concerning Matthew 8:12 and Matthew 22:13, you must remember that the interpretation in these passages is to the nation of Israel first of all. And secondarily, the principle can also be applied to believers. It is true that believers will be judged for their works at the judgment seat of Christ, which will not be a pleasant experience, according to I Corinthians 3, and II Corinthians 5:10.

210. Does Not Matthew 10:28 Teach Final Annihilation?

> And fear not them which kill the body, but are not able to kill the soul: but rather fear him which is able to destroy both soul and body in hell (Matt. 10:28).

I fear that your doubting friend fails to distinguish between destruction and annihilation. There is nothing in the entire Bible that either the body or soul is going to be annihilated. The word, "destroy," in Scripture does not necessarily mean to "pass out of existence." For instance, I can take my watch which runs perfectly now, and dash it upon the pavement, and I thereby destroy the watch. It is spoiled for the purpose for which it was made, but I have not annihilated the watch. The parts are all still there. In the same way, God created man for His own fellowship, but through sin, God is going to destroy the sinner, not annihilate him. That is, he will be spoiled for the fellowship of God, and will have to spend eternity in hell, outside of the presence of God. Certainly the book of Revelation is pefectly clear that the wicked will not be annihilated, but will be tormented day and night forever and ever.

211. Does Matthew 12:36-37 Teach That Jokes Are Sin?

> But I say unto you, That every idle word that men shall speak, they shall give account thereof in the day of judgment.
>
> For by thy words thou shalt be justified, and by thy words thou shalt be condemned (Matt. 12:36-37).

In regard to "idle words" mentioned in Matthew 12, I believe that the Lord here wishes to place the emphasis on the word, "idle"; that is, "meaningless, and useless jesting and frivolity," which have no connection at all with our spiritual life. Of course, I realize that the Lord has given to us a sense of humor, and while the days are exceedingly solemn, we also recognize that young people are not fully conscious of the gravity of the days in which we are living.

I take it that Jesus is speaking here especially about foolish jesting which has no place in the Christian life. However, for children and young folks to have a good time, and to indulge in a certain amount of humor, certainly that cannot be contrary to the Scriptures. We cannot make old men and old women out of young folks. As they grow up, they usually develop a more serious attitude. However, I quite agree with you, that we as children of God should be exceedingly solemn in these days, and not spend our time in useless jesting and joking which can only minister to the flesh, and have no bearing upon our spiritual life.

I personally wish that our young people could be more serious in their thinking, in the light of all the conditions which are in the world round about us.

212. Does Leaven Refer to the Gospel in Matthew 13?

The parable of the leaven in Matthew 13 is one of the parables of the Kingdom of Heaven. This does not mean "heaven," but applies to the professing sphere of Christendom. This is apparent when you realize that in the second parable both tares and wheat grow up together, and in the last parable there are both good and bad fish in the net.

Leaven represents the evil both in doctrine and practice which is introduced into professing Christendom during this age. Professing Christendom is quite another thing than the body of Christ. In professing Christendom, we have both born-again believers and unregenerates. Hence, the leaven does its work.

213. Does Matthew 13:15 Teach That God Blinds the Eyes of Sinners So They Cannot Believe on Him?

> For this people's heart is waxed gross, and their ears are dull of hearing, and their eyes they have closed; lest at any time they should see with their eyes and hear with their ears, and should understand with their heart, and should be converted, and I should heal them (Matt. 13:15).

In regard to your question concerning Matthew 13:15, you must remember that he is speaking here about Israel, who was blinded in order that the Gentiles might, through the rejection of Israel, be brought to a saving knowledge of the Lord Jesus Christ. In this connection you ought to read carefully the 11th chapter of Romans, which also tells us the reason. In the 11th chapter of Romans, especially verses 7 to 12, we have the explanation of Matthew 13:15, where we are told that Israel was rejected that the fulness of the Gentiles might be brought in. This is a deep mystery, but it gives us a glimpse into the eternal counsels of God.

214. What Do You Understand By the "Keys of the Kingdom" As Mentioned in Matthew 16:19?

You must notice first of all that these keys are "plural", and that there are more than one. Secondly, you must notice that they were given to Peter alone. And finally, they are not called the keys of the "church" or the keys of "heaven" but the keys of the *Kingdom of Heaven*. Peter used these keys (three in number) on three occasions.

1. On Pentecost Peter was God's man to open the gospel to the nation of Israel.
2. The second use of the keys was in Acts 8:14-15 when the door of the gospel was opened to the Samaritans.
3. The third use of the keys occurred in Acts 10 when in the household of Cornelius, Peter opens the door of the gospel to the Gentiles.

All of this was according to Christ's order, "beginning at Jerusalem, and all Judea, and Samaria, and to the uttermost parts of the earth." Peter having completed the use of the keys in Acts 10, now passes out of the scene and Paul, the apostle of the Gentiles, takes his place.

215. Can Faith Remove Literal Mountains, As Taught in Matthew 17:20?

> And Jesus said unto them, Because of your unbelief: for verily I say unto you, If ye have faith as a grain of mustard seed, ye shall say unto this mountain, Remove hence to yonder place; and it shall remove; and nothing shall be impossible unto you (Matt. 17:20).

Yes, I believe in taking this verse in Matthew 17:20 literally. I believe with all my heart that if we had enough faith we would be able to move literal mountains if it was for the glory of God. Of course, we must remember that merely moving mountains for the sake of making a demonstration is not pleasing to the Lord, but if it is to His glory and for the help of others, I believe it would be possible. There is also a spiritual application which means that if we had faith, no matter how great our troubles may be, even though they be as great as mountains, the Lord is able to remove them when we are willing to trust Him.

216. Does Matthew 18:15-17 Apply to the Church or Israel?

Moreover if thy brother shall trespass against thee, go and tell him his fault between thee and him alone: if he shall hear thee, thou hast gained thy brother.

But if he will not hear thee, then take with thee one or two more, that in the mouth of two or three witnesses every word may be established.

And if he shall neglect to hear them, tell it unto the church: but if he neglect to hear the church, let him be unto thee as an heathen man and a publican (Matt. 18:15-17).

I firmly believe that this passage applies to the Church of today, since our Lord in this passage is making known the first reference to the mystery of the Church. (See verse 17.) If this order were followed, it would prevent much trouble in the church today.

217. Can We Receive Anything for Which We Ask, If We Follow Matthew 18:19?

Again I say unto you, That if two of you shall agree on earth as touching any thing that they shall ask, it shall be done for them of my Father which is in heaven (Matt. 18:19).

Jesus here is speaking about the ministry of believers, especially in the assembly. If we ask anything in the name of the Lord Jesus, and agree with some other believer and trust the Lord, He gives us what we ask for upon one condition; namely, that we ask according to His will. It is possible for Christians to ask for things which are not according to God's will, and this promise in Matthew 18 is dependent upon the other conditions laid down in God's Word.

218. Does the Parable of the Vineyard in Matthew 20 Apply to the Church Today?

In regard to your question concerning the parable of the vineyard in Matthew 20, there are two schools of interpretation on this particular passage. It is not an easy one. However, when we remember that Matthew is the gospel of the Kingdom, and most of it refers to the nation of Israel rather than to the Church, we have every reason to believe that this can by interpretation be applied to the nation, rather than to the Church. The other interpretation, of course, is that the parables of the Lord Jesus Christ refer to this present dispensation while the Lord of the Harvest Himself is absent. I rather feel that both of them are in view in this passage.

Primarily, this undoubtedly refers to the period of time after the Rapture of the Church, and has to do with the nation of Israel in the land, rather than the Church. This I believe to be the primary interpretation. However, we must remember that there are also secondary applications, and that there is an application here for the Church of the Lord Jesus Christ as well. As another example of this, you will recall that Christ said that two should be grinding at the mill, one should be taken and the other left. Here again the interpretation is to the nation of Israel at the end of the tribulation, but by application it is also true of the Rapture of the Church.

219. In Matthew 20:16 Who Are the First Who Shall Be Last?

> So the last shall be first, and the first last: for many be called, but few chosen   (Matt. 20:16).

"The first shall be last" in this passage deals with the sovereignty of God, as it is apparent from the parable of the vineyard. Verse 15 will explain this. The Lord can do as He pleases with His creature. Those who are first in this life will be last in the life to come.

220. Does Matthew 22:14 Teach "Election"?

> For many are called, but few are chosen (Matt. 22:14).

In this verse we have reference made to the two great facts of Scripture; first, the sovereignty of God in election;

and second, the free will of man in believing. It is true that the call goes out to all, but only those who are chosen will believe. This rests, of course, upon the foreknowledge of God according to I Peter 1:2, "Elect according to the foreknowledge of God the Father."

221. Please Explain the Meaning of the Man Without A Wedding Garment in Matthew 22:11.

> And when the king came in to see the guests, he saw there a man which had not on a wedding garment (Matt. 22:11).

The man without the wedding garment was a professing believer without being truly regenerated. He tried to come to the wedding in his own self-righteous clothing and was promptly rejected.

222. In Matthew 22:28, 30 Jesus Says We Will Be As the Angels in Heaven. Will We Actually Be Angels and Not Know Our Husbands and Wives in Heaven?

> Therefore in the resurrection whose wife shall she be of the seven? for they all had her.
>
> For in the resurrection they neither marry, nor are given in marriage, but are as the angels of God in heaven (Matt. 22:28, 30).

In this passage, remember the setting. The question was "marriage in heaven." The Sadducees had, of course, given a hypothetical question concerning a woman who had had seven husbands. Now this does not teach in any sense whatsoever that we are going to be angels when we get to heaven. It merely indicates that in heaven our relationship to Christ and one to another will be on so much higher a plane than the relationship of marriage here upon the earth, that we shall lose the lesser relationship in the higher, in the presence of the Lord Jesus Christ. There is nothing in the Bible to indicate that we are going to be angels. In fact, we are told that we shall judge angels. We are also told that the angels are our ministers, appointed to serve us, according to Hebrews chapter 2. We shall always continue to be human beings, and at the resurrection we shall receive bodies, human bodies, glorified and eternal, to be sure, but human bodies, just like the body of the Lord Jesus Christ at His resurrection.

Therefore, the 30th verse speaks of believers in the resurrection, not believers now before the resurrection. Please note carefully. Jesus says, "In the resurrection, they neither marry." There will be no marriage after the resurrection, but we will be as the angels of God, who of course, never marry. This does not mean, however, that we will not remember our previous relationships, and praise God for all the experiences we have had here upon the earth.

223. Matthew 23:9 — Why Is It Wrong to Call Anyone Father?

>   And call no man your father upon the earth: for one is your Father, which is in heaven (Matt. 23:9).

In regard to Matthew 23:9, the reference here is definitely to religious life, and I do not believe that it applies to family life. To call anyone else father in the spiritual sense is to deny the spiritual Fatherhood of God. For this reason the Catholic Church is in error. However, in the family relations, whether the word, "papa," or "sire," or "father" is used, there is no intention of ascribing to him spiritual fatherhood. It also says that we are to call no one "master," and yet we call everyone "mister" which is only a variation of "master." You will see from this that the difference lies in using it in a church sense or in the relationship of the home. Certainly the Catholic priest is not a father even in the latter sense.

224. In Matthew 24:19-20, What Is the Meaning of "Woe Unto Them That Are with Child and Give Suck in Those Days?"

In regard to Matthew 24:19-20, remember Jesus is talking about the tribulation and especially as it affects the Jewish people in Palestine. It has no application whatsoever to the Church which shall be taken out before the tribulation begins.

225. Will the Church Pass Through the Tribulation According to Matthew 24:20?

> But pray ye that your flight be not in the winter, neither on the sabbath day (Matt. 24:20).

If we will only remember to "rightly divide the Word of truth," and remember the dispensational truth, we will have no trouble with this passage. Matthew 24 has absolutely nothing to do with the Church, but deals entirely with the nation of Israel. The Church will not go through the tribulation, and since Matthew 24 deals exclusively with the tribulation period, it has to do only with the Jewish people whose capitol is Jerusalem, and whose land is Palestine. As a result of this, the entire location of this passage is Palestine, and has to do with God's ancient nation of Israel in the tribulation period. Since the sabbath was given to Israel but never to the Gentiles, it is mentioned here and has absolutely no bearing on the sabbath in this dispensation. If we rightly divide the Word of truth, and separate between the Church and Israel, and remember that the Church is gone in Matthew 24, and that God is dealing here with the ancient covenant nation, we will have no difficulty whatsoever.

226. What Is "The Generation Which Shall Not Pass" in Matthew 24:34?

> Verily I say unto you, This generation shall not pass, till all these things be fulfilled (Matt. 24:34).

I agree with Scofield that the word, "generation," "genea," refers to the nation of Israel as it does elsewhere in Scripture, and what Jesus is saying is that the nation of Israel will never perish or pass away until all the things prophesied in Matthew have been fulfilled. Although some Bible teachers claim that it refers to this present living generation, I believe this is an error. In fact, this was taught some forty years ago and that generation is already gone. To say that it would occur during any particular living generation comes close to setting dates for the coming of the Lord, which is unscriptural.

227. Was the Servant in Matthew 25 Who Hid His One Talent a Saved Believer?

The servants in this particular parable were undoubtedly all saved, although I must admit that it is pretty hard to associate the "gnashing of teeth" with it. However, when we look at it in the light of the judgment seat of Christ, I think we can find that there will be some unhappy experiences when the Lord comes to judge His saints. In the light of I Corinthians 3:11-15, I think this passage can be explained as referring to believers who will receive no rewards.

228. Who Are the Sheep and the Goats in Matthew 25:31-46?

I must frankly admit to you that this is one of the most difficult prophetic passages in the entire Scriptures. Most fundamental Bible teachers, together with Dr. Scofield, tell us that this is the judgment of the nations at the end of the tribulation period, and that the brethren mentioned in verse 40 are the nation of Israel. However, there are too many questions left unanswered by such an interpretation. I shall need more light on this passage before I feel that I am in a position to speak with any sense of authority. The moral lessons here are easy to find — that we should be kind and charitable in the light of the coming judgment; that rewards and punishment will be determined in a degree at least by our conduct here below. When I come to a passage which I do not clearly see, I usually let it rest until I receive more definite light.

229. Was David Among Those Raised from the Dead in Matthew 27:52-53?

> And the graves were opened; and many bodies of the saints which slept arose,
>
> And came out of the graves after his resurrection, and went into the holy city, and appeared unto many (Matt. 27:52-53).

In regard to your question concerning the resurrection of David, if you will carefully read the 27th chapter of Matthew, verses 52 and 53, you will notice that it does not say that *all* the saints of the Old Testament arose, but it says definitely, "*many* bodies of the saints which slept arose." This, of course, implies that they did not *all* come out. This resurrection of a company at the resurrection of Christ are the "firstfruits from among the dead." The harvest will not come until the second coming of Christ in the rapture. You probably are familiar with the fact that in the Old Testament there was a feast of firstfruits, and then a harvest festival. The selected company in Matthew 27 represent the firstfruits.

David was definitely not among that company, for the Apostle Peter tells us in Acts 2:29, "Men and brethren, let me freely speak unto you of the patriarch David, that he is both dead and buried, and his sepulchre is with us unto this day." This definitely states that David was dead at the time that Peter preached at Pentecost, fifty days after the events of Matthew 27. Since there has been no resurrection since that time, David must, of course, still be in the grave. (See also Acts 2:34).

230. Why Was Mary Forbidden to Touch Jesus after His Resurrection, and Yet the Women Held His Feet in Matthew 28:9?

Between the time the Lord Jesus forbade Mary to touch Him, and this incident in Matthew 28:8-9, the Lord must of necessity have ascended into heaven as He told Mary. You remember He said to Mary, "touch Me not, for I am not yet ascended unto my Father." So there is only one explanation. In the interval between the two incidents, the Lord Jesus Christ must have fulfilled this statement, and have ascended unto the Father.

231. Why Did Jesus Charge People Not to Tell Others of His Miracles, As in Mark 5:43?

> And he charged them straitly that no man should know it; and commanded that something should be given her to eat (Mark 5:43).

In regard to Mark 5:41-43, you must remember that when the Lord came the first time, He came to be rejected, and therefore, He made Himself known to those who believed on Him, but hid Himself from those who were His enemies. It was God's purpose and will that Christ should go to the Cross, and so according to Romans 11, the eyes of Israel were blinded so that they would not believe on Him.

232. Who Are the Children and Who Are the Dogs in Mark 7:27-28?

> But Jesus said unto her, Let the children first be filled: for it is not meet to take the children's bread, and to cast it unto the dogs.
> And she answered and said unto him, Yes, Lord: yet the dogs under the table eat of the children's crumbs (Mark 7:27-28).

You must again realize that Jesus came first of all to offer the Kingdom to the nation of Israel. Only after they had rejected Him, and turned down the King, is the Gospel to go to the Gentiles. The children in verse 27 of Mark 7 are the Jewish people, and the Gentiles here are called "dogs." That was a common expression among Israel, to call the Gentiles "dogs." This woman in Mark 7 realized that Christ came not only to offer Himself as the King of Israel, but also to be the Saviour of the Gentiles. Her answer in verse 28 the Lord marvelled at and recognized by healing her daughter. I hope that this explains your problem.

233. What Is the Baptism in Mark 10:38-39?

But Jesus said unto them, Ye know not what ye ask: can ye drink of the cup that I drink of? and be baptized with the baptism that I am baptized with?

And they said unto him, We can. And Jesus said unto them, Ye shall indeed drink of the cup that I drink of; and with the baptism that I am baptized withal shall ye be baptized (Mark 10:38-39).

This refers to the passion and death of the Lord Jesus Christ, the same as the cup. Baptism is a symbol of the death and resurrection of our Lord, and this baptism also refers to His death on the Cross of Calvary.

234. Are the Signs in Mark 16:15-18, Such As Healing, Handling of Snakes, etc. for This Dispensation?

And he said unto them, Go ye into all the world, and preach the gospel to every creature.

He that believeth and is baptized shall be saved; but he that believeth not shall be damned.

And these signs shall follow them that believe; In my name shall they cast out devils; they shall speak with new tongues;

They shall take up serpents; and if they drink any deadly thing, it shall not hurt them; they shall lay hands on the sick, and they shall recover (Mark 16:15-18).

This, of course, is a rather difficult passage, but I believe that when we learn to rightly divide the Word of truth, we should have no difficulty at all. I believe that verses 15 and 16 are a general commission which the Lord Jesus Christ gave unto us for this entire dispensation. However, the verses 17 and 18, which have to do with the signs of the apostleship, were for a particular period only. I fully realize the fact that God is able today to do the same miracles and signs which Jesus did while He was here upon the earth. It is not a question of God's ability. It is a question of the program of God. We believe that signs and miracles which were performed by Jesus and the disciples were for a specific time and a definite age, before the New Testament was completed. They were the evidence and the truth of the ministry of Christ and of the disciples. However, after the canon of Scripture was completed and all the books of the New Testament had been written, God expects us to believe His promises rather than to look for signs and miracles, so we believe that today signs and miracles as recorded in the 16th of Mark are past, generally speaking, and we are today to believe the record that God has given concerning His Son. Whenever it pleases the Lord to perform these miracles or to give these gifts, He is still able to do so. We do not believe, however, that they are the rule for this dispensation. If God chooses to heal men without any physical means He is able to do it, and often does. I do not believe that we ought to tempt God by taking up rattle snakes or by drinking poison just in order to test the Word of God. That is presumption, and is tempting the Almighty and God cannot be tempted. I want to repeat, that I do not want to limit the power of God. He can do anything He pleases, but we are to remember that nothing pleases Him more than when His children are willing to trust His Word and His promises without any other evidence whatsoever. If Mark 16:15-18 is all for us, then it must always succeed, and such is not the case, as you will soon find out, if you drink poison and handle snakes.

235. Does Mark 16:16 Teach That Baptism Is Necessary to Be Saved?

He that believeth and is baptized shall be saved; but he that believeth not shall be damned (Mark 16:16).

In Mark 16:16 you must remember here that the Lord says, "He that believeth and is baptized shall be saved," but the next phrase says, "He that believeth not shall be damned." The "baptism" is left out in this last phrase, thereby indicating that it is in harmony with the rest of Scripture, that while baptism is an institution of the Lord, it is not essential for salvation.

236. Can We Compel Men to Be Saved According to Luke 14:23?

And the lord said unto the servant, Go out into the highways and hedges, and compel them to come in, that my house may be filled (Luke 14:23).

In regard to your question concerning Luke 14:23, the word, "compel" is "anagkazo" which means "to urgently insist" rather than to force.

237. Does Luke 14:26 Teach Us Actually to Hate Our Parents?

If any man come to me, and hate not his father, and mother, and wife, and children, and brethren, and sisters, yea, and his own life also, he cannot be my disciple (Luke 14:26).

The word, "hate," in Luke 14:26 is a comparative word in the Greek and not an absolute word. It means that the tender love we have for our fathers and mothers and loved ones is like hatred *in comparison* with the love that we have for the Lord Jesus Christ. The Lord certainly does not tell us to hate our loved ones.

238. Please Explain the Parable of the Wise Steward in Luke 16.

In regard to Luke 16:1-12, the entire passage deals with making provision for the future, and if the worldly steward wisely made provision for his future, so we are, above all things, to make provision for our spiritual future.

239. What Does It Mean, "The Kingdom of God Cometh Not by Observation," In Luke 17:20 and John 18:36?

And when he was demanded of the Pharisees, when the kingdom of God should come, he answered them and said, The kingdom of God cometh not with observation (Luke 17:20).

Jesus answered, My kingdom is not of this world: if my kingdom were of this world, then would my servants fight, that I should not be delivered to the Jews: but now is my kingdom not from hence (John 18:36).

In regard to Luke 17:20, the word, "observation" means "pomp" or "show." The Lord is saying that when the Kingdom comes, it will not be in the way that the earthly kingdoms are set up. The fact was that the King was already in the midst of His people, and therefore, the Lord said, "the kingdom is among you"; that is, in the person of the King.

The same is true of John 18:36. The word, "world," is "aeon," and means "age," and what Jesus said was, "My kingdom is not of this age," thereby implying that His kingdom *would* be set up.

240. Did Jesus Make Intoxicating Wine in His First Miracle in John 2:1-12?

In regard to the miracle of making water into wine, there is, of course, no record that Jesus drank any Himself. However, the point in the miracle is entirely overlooked when we confine our thoughts to what kind of wine this might have been. The real point of the whole miracle is found in John 2:11 —

This beginning of miracles did Jesus in Cana of Galilee, and manifested forth his glory; and his disciples believed on him.

There is nothing that pleases the enemy more than that we should quibble about the details and forget the purpose for which the miracle was performed. The word for "wine" in this passage is the same word used elsewhere for "fermented wine."

241. What Is the Water Referred to in John 3:5, "Born of Water"?

Jesus answered, Verily, verily, I say unto thee, Except a man be born of water and of the Spirit, he cannot enter into the kingdom of God (John 3:5).

I am quite familiar with the interpretations of the "water" in John 3. Some claim it is literal water, some claim it is the first, natural birth. However, I am sure that if you will refer to the following passages, you will see that it is the Word which regenerates: I Peter 1:23; Ephesians 5:26; John 15:3; John 17:17.

In all these passages you will notice that the Word regenerates, cleanses us, and is called the "washing of the water by the Word." However, when we get to heaven we will know about all these things more clearly than here. John 3:5 means that we are born again by the Spirit applying the Word of God to our hearts.

242. Please Explain "Worshipping in Spirit and in Truth" As Stated in John 4:24.

God is a Spirit: and they that worship him must worship him in spirit and in truth (John 4:24).

In regard to your question concerning John 4:24, Jesus is teaching that the place where we worship makes no difference, but our attitude of spirit and sincerity of heart are the important things. Whether we worship one place or another makes no difference with the Lord, as long as we are truthful and sincere.

243. Are There Passages in the Bible Which Are Not the Word of God, But Were Added by the Translators, such as John 5:3-4?

I am quite familiar with the general interpretation of the passage in John 5, as well as the one in the 8th of Acts. However, I have disregarded in my own personal ministry all of these attempts to explain the reason why some of these verses seem to have been omitted from some of the original manuscripts. The original manuscripts of the Bible, both the Old and New Testaments, have never been found. We have our translation of the Scriptures from other manuscripts which were copies of the original, so that it is the safest thing to go by our translation as we have it. If we allow one man to take out a verse here, and another one there, there is no end to the confusion which may result. I, therefore, accept the entire record of the moving of the water including verses 3 and 4, as well as the passages which you mentioned. In this way there is no doubt left in the mind. After all, even omitting verses 3 and 4 of John 5 does not alter the fact that there was a supernatural and miraculous action in this. The Lord Jesus Christ Himself did not in any way seek to correct this so-called superstition. Pay no attention at all to those places where certain passages of the Scripture are said to have been inserted or added. If we are to begin along this line, there is no end to the confusion which will result.

244. Does John 5:24 and 29 Teach That We Are Saved by Doing Good Deeds?

Verily, verily, I say unto you, He that heareth my word, and believeth on him that sent me, hath everlasting life, and shall not come into condemnation; but is passed from death unto life.

And shall come forth; they that have done good, unto the
resurrection of life; and they that have done evil, unto
the resurrection of damnation (John 5:24, 29).

Your question concerning the two verses in John 5 are
explained in John 6:29, "Jesus answered and said unto
them, This is the work of God, that ye believe on him
whom he hath sent." The ones who have done good in
verse 29 of John 5, have done so by believing on the
Lord Jesus Christ. Those who have not believed have done
evil. Jesus said in John 16 that the Spirit would convict the world of sin because they believed not. The only
sin which condemns is unbelief. In John 6:29 we are told
that this is the *work* of God, "that ye believe on Him whom
He hath sent."

245. How Was Jesus Glorified and When? — John 7:39

(But this spake he of the Spirit, which they that believe
on him should receive: for the Holy Ghost was not yet
given; because that Jesus was not yet glorified) (John 7:39).

In regard to your question concerning the fulfillment of
John 7:39, there is a great diversity of opinion among
Bible students. Some believe that He was glorified on the
Cross, others that when He ascended into the Father's
presence on the resurrection day, and others that when He
went in the ascension forty days later. There seems to
be no agreement in the matter, and it is one of those things
we will have to wait for until we meet the Lord Jesus Christ
in the glory. That will be one of the thrills of eternity,
when we find out so many things which are not clear here
below.

246. Does John 9:1-3 Teach That a Man Can Sin Before He Is Born?

And as Jesus passed by, he saw a man which was blind
from his birth.

And his disciples asked him, saying, Master, who did
sin, this man, or his parents, that he was born blind?

Jesus answered, Neither hath this man sinned, nor his parents: but that the works of God should be made manifest in him (John 9:1-3).

The question of the disciples, "Who hath sinned, this man or his parents?" shows the foolishness of some theological thinking. The question as the disciples put it was just a foolish question with no Scriptural basis whatsoever. It demonstrates to what peculiar conclusions unscriptural theology will lead a man. The answer of Jesus is quite clear that the blindness was neither the sin of the victim nor his parents, but the foreknown will of God in order that He might exhibit His power.

247. Does John 10:9 Teach the Falling from Grace of Believers? They Are Said "To Go In and Out."

I am the door: by me if any man enter in, he shall be saved, and shall go in and out, and find pasture (John 10:9).

The passage in John 10:9 speaks of the liberty we have in Christ, going in and out, and the 16th verse refers to the sheep of the Church, as in contrast to the sheep of Israel. The "going in and out" speaks of service and of the liberty we have. However, in going in and out, we do not have to pass over the wall, but we go in and out through the Lord Jesus Christ, who is the Door. If you will distinguish between our *position* in Christ, as being safe in Him, and our *liberty* in Christ, in going in and out for service and bringing others in, I think this matter will become clear to you.

248. In John 12:31-32 Jesus Says "When I Am Lifted Up I Will Draw All Men Unto Me." Does This Refer to Lifting Up Christ in Our Preaching?

Now is the judgment of this world: now shall the prince of this world be cast out.

And I, if I be lifted up from the earth, will draw all men unto me (John 12:31-32).

No, in regard to John 12:31-32, the 32nd verse clearly indicates that Jesus was speaking of His death upon the Cross, for He said, "when I be lifted up." On the Cross Satan was judged, and the sentence passed, but the judgment will not be executed fully until the Second Coming of Christ.

249. John 14:12

> Verily, verily, I say unto you, He that believeth on me, the works that I do shall he do also; and greater works than these shall he do; because I go unto my Father.

This verse looks forward to the day of Pentecost, when the Lord said that "greater things than He had done, would be done through the Church," and was referring to the period of time in which we are now living during which the Gospel is going out in the power of the Holy Spirit. When the Lord Jesus was here, the Spirit had not yet been poured out upon the Church, and so He gave them the promise that they should receive power after that the Holy Ghost was given unto them. This does not refer to miracles and signs and wonders, but rather to the power of the Gospel which is the business of the Church of Jesus Christ today. This is the way that I understand the verse.

250. John 14:15

> If ye love me, keep my commandments (John 14:15).

In regard to John 14:15 remember that when Jesus speaks about His commandments as "My commandments" He does not necessarily refer to the Ten commandments of Moses. In I John 3:23 we read this: "And this is His commandment, that we should believe on the Name of His Son, Jesus Christ, and love one another as He gave us commandment." You will see from this that Christ was evidently not referring to the Ten Commandments, but to the higher law of love, which He expects of His children.

251. In John 15, Does Jesus Teach That Saved People Can Be Lost Again?

No. In regard to your question concerning John 15, you must remember that Jesus is talking here about fruit-bearing, and not primarily about salvation itself. The branches are all saved people and the Lord Jesus here tells us that He will judge those who do not bear fruit.

In studying the 15th chapter of John, we must remember that Christ is teaching the truth of fruit-bearing. It has nothing to do with falling from grace but fruit-bearing is the burden of this passage. The fruitless branches are still branches, but shall be saved so as by fire. It says in verse 2, "every branch *in me* which beareth not fruit."

This chapter is not written to prove a doctrine, but to inspire service. It is not a matter of salvation, but entirely a matter of fruit-bearing and rewards.

252. Does Not John 15:6 Refute the Doctrine of Eternal Security?

If a man abide not in me, he is cast forth as a branch, and is withered; and men gather them, and cast them into the fire, and they are burned (John 15:6).

No. The sixth verse of John 15 has to be taken in connection with verse 2, and we must remember that the branch is still in Him, but is fruitless. Since there is no fruit, men condemn them, but according to verse 6, they are still branches. In verse 6, he is cast forth *as a branch*. That has reference to the judgment seat of Christ. Study John 15:16 in the light of I Corinthians 3:15.

253. Why Is Judas Called the "Son of Perdition" in John 17:12?

While I was with them in the world, I kept them in thy name: those that thou gavest me I have kept, and none of them is lost, but the son of perdition; that the scripture might be fulfilled (John 17:12).

In the passage from John 17 which you quote, Jesus called Judas the Son of Perdition. By referring to II Thessalonians 2, you will notice that the antichrist is also called "the son of perdition." In both cases the definite article, "the," is used. It is also said that Judas was a devil, and it is generally understood that Judas was an attempt on the part of Satan to produce the personal antichrist, and that the Man of Sin who will appear on the earth after the Church is raptured will be Judas resurrected again.

254. Does John 20:22-23 Teach That the Disciples Received the Holy Spirit Before Pentecost?

And when he had said this, he breathed on them, and saith unto them, Receive ye the Holy Ghost:

Whose soever sins ye remit, they are remitted unto them; and whose soever sins ye retain, they are retained (John 20:22-23).

No. In John 20:22 the words of our Lord, "Receive ye the Holy Ghost," undoubtedly look forward to the day of Pentecost. It does not say that they received the Holy Ghost at that particular time, but He said, "receive ye the Holy Ghost."

Remember that in John 20 the Lord Jesus Christ gives the promise of the Holy Ghost. There is no record that the Holy Ghost was poured upon them at that particular time. He merely said, "receive ye the Holy Ghost." This promise in John 20 was fulfilled in the second chapter of Acts in the outpouring of the Holy Spirit.

255. Can Sins Be Remitted by Men? John 20:23.

In regard to "the remission of sin" in verse 23 of John 20, this, of course, has reference to all who preach the Gospel of God's grace. When we preach the Gospel, the sins are remitted of those who believe. All those who reject that Gospel retain their sin. In that sense, everyone who preaches the Gospel has the power to remit and to retain sin. It is not in any sense limited to the apostles or to any particular individual.

256. What Is the Difference Between the Baptism Unto Repentance in Acts 2:38 and Christian Baptism?

> Then Peter said unto them, Repent, and be baptized every one of you in the name of Jesus Christ for the remission of sins, and ye shall receive the gift of the Holy Ghost (Acts 2:38).

You must remember that in the second chapter of Acts, there were no Gentiles, but there were only Jews and proselytes. The baptism Peter offers here is the baptism of regeneration which belongs to the kingdom age, and not to this age of grace. After Israel rejected the offer of the kingdom in Acts 7, the Gospel goes to the Gentiles, and Christian baptism comes in, as we find in the household of Cornelius, Lydia and the Philippian jailor. The baptism in Acts 2 was essential to have sins forgiven. Christian baptism is a testimony that our sins have been forgiven.

257. Acts 8 and 18 — Must the Believer Receive Signs and Miracles to Know That He Is Saved?

In regard to your question concerning Acts 8 and Acts 18, where faith was not accompanied by the receiving of the Holy Spirit when they believed, you must remember that Peter had committed to him the Keys to the Kingdom. He exercised them first of all at Pentecost when he opened the door of the Kingdom to the Jews. Then he exercised the use of these keys once again in the household of Cornelius because he was a Gentile, but in the case of Acts 8, it was not one of the apostles, but Philip, and since it was the apostolic work to open the door, as evidenced by the giving of the Holy Spirit, the apostles from Jerusalem had to come down, and in Acts 18, of course, we have the Apostle Paul. The gifts of the Holy Spirit in the book

of Acts were given because the Scriptures were not yet
fully completed, and they were evidences and signs of the
authority in which they were given. In the second chapter
of Acts we read that the signs and miracles which Jesus
performed were the evidence and the approval of His
God-sent ministry. The same thing is repeated again concerning the apostles in Hebrews 2:3,4. Now that the Holy
Spirit has been given and the Scriptures are complete, we
are shut up to faith, and are not to look for anything besides just simply believing and trusting the Word of God.

258. Does the Expression, "And Thy House," in Acts 16:31 Teach That There Were Babies in This Home?

In regard to the phrase, "believe on the Lord Jesus
Christ and thou shalt be saved, and thy house," the "house"
refers, of course, to the members of the family who can
be saved by believing, just exactly the same way as the
Philippian jailor himself. In other words, Paul says,
"Believe on the Lord Jesus Christ, and *thou* shalt be
saved," and this also applies to your house. They can be
saved through faith, and faith alone. Evidently all the
members in the jailor's house were old enough to believe.
The Christian has a right to claim his family for God.

259. Some Jewish Workers Claim That Romans 1:16 Teaches That We Should Preach the Gospel and Give Our Money to Jewish Missions Before Any Other Work. Is This Scriptural?

> For I am not ashamed of the gospel of Christ: for it is
> the power of God unto salvation to every one that believeth;
> to the Jew first, and also to the Greek.

No. We must remember that the injunction, "to the Jew
first, and also to the Greek," was dispensational and is
historical. It is true that the Gospel went first to Jerusalem
and all Judea, and then when the nation of Israel rejected
it, it went to the Gentiles as it is going today. There is
nothing in Scripture to indicate that we must give the Jew

the Gospel first in this dispensation before we give it to the Gentile. Today there is no difference; all have sinned and need the same message, and come by faith to the same Christ. We believe in giving the Gospel to the Jew, but no more so than to the Gentile. "To the Jew first," was fulfilled in Acts.

260. Can the Heathen Be Saved Without the Gospel? Please Explain Romans 1:19-20.

Because that which may be known of God is manifest in them; for God hath shewed it unto them.

For the invisible things of him from the creation of the world are clearly seen, being understood by the things that are made, even his eternal power and Godhead; so that they are without excuse (Romans 1:19-20).

In regard to your question concerning Romans 1:19-20, the Bible is plain that there can be no salvation apart from faith in the Lord Jesus Christ. Faith in the God of creation is not enough. However, we must remember that God is a just and righteous God, and that the heathen who have never heard the Gospel will be judged by the light which they had. The judgment of the heathen will be infinitely lighter than that of those who have heard the Word and then rejected it. There will be degrees of punishment as well as degrees of rewards for saints.

261. Can Anyone Believe Without the Spirit, or Is Believing Already the Result of the Operation of God in Salvation? I Refer to Romans 3:11.

There is none that understandeth, there is none that seeketh after God (Romans 3:11).

The Bible teaches the total depravity of man, and that man without the operation of the Holy Spirit never seeks after God. He may seek after *a* God; he may seek after religion, but he does not seek after the true God. Ephesians 2:8 tells us plainly, "For by grace are ye saved through

faith, and that not of yourselves; *it is the gift of God.*"
This is the condition of the human heart, and if Jesus had
not come into the world to seek and to save that which was
lost, and the Holy Spirit would not move upon the hearts of
men, all would be lost.

262. What Is Meant by the Phrase in Romans 3:25, "Remission of Sins That Are Past"?

Concerning the expression, "the remission of sins that
are past," this refers to the sins which were committed
before the Cross of Calvary, when the Lord Jesus Christ
made full atonement for the sins that are past. You realize,
of course, that the blood of bulls and of goats, and the
sacrifices of the Old Testament could only cover sin, but
could not in any sense take away sins. This could only
be done by the blood of the Lord Jesus Christ. So up until
the Cross, God did on the promisory note of the Lord Jesus
Christ, remit sins, but they were not completely put out of
the way until the blood was shed on the Cross of Calvary.

263. Does Romans 10:9 Teach Two Different Plans of Salvation, One for the Jew and Another for the Gentile?

> That if thou shalt confess with thy mouth the Lord Jesus,
> and shalt believe in thine heart that God hath raised him
> from the dead, thou shalt be saved (Romans 10:9).

In regard to your comment concerning the quotation of
Romans 10:9, I am thoroughly familiar with the interpretation which you are using. In fact, it is quite commonly accepted among a certain group. However, I have al-
ways felt that the 10th of Romans deals with this present
dispensation, while I realize that Romans 9, 10, and 11
have to do with the Jewish nation. In Romans 9 we have
Israel's past history. In Romans 10 we have Israel's
present condition. In Romans 11 we have Israel's future
restoration. This comes as a parenthesis in the book of
Romans, of course.

However, in Romans 10 we have God's word in regard to the present condition of the nation of Israel during this time of dispersion and setting aside. This, therefore, is the plan of salvation at this time, and since there is no different plan for the Jew than for the Gentile, I take it that Romans 10:9 applies to all men during this period between Israel's national rejection and their restoration again. How wonderful it will be when we get to glory, and will have all of these problems answered!

264. According to Romans 10:17, Is It True That One Can Be Saved Only by "Hearing" the Word?

> So then faith cometh by hearing, and hearing by the word of God (Romans 10:17).

In regard to your question concerning the result of salvation by the spoken word, it has always been my contention, based upon the Word of God, that it is the spoken word which God uses to convict the souls of men. True, printed literature is valuable as an aid in preparing hearts for salvation, but we believe that "faith cometh by hearing, and hearing by the Word of God." I have not been able to find a single instance in all my experience of anyone who was ever saved without having heard at least something of the Word of God spoken by another. Of course, in the case of folk who cannot hear, God always has a special dispensation.

265. What Is Meant by the "Wild Branches" of the Olive Tree in Romans 11?

In Romans 11, Paul is speaking of Israel as the olive tree, and the church as the Body of Christ in this dispensation. The root of the tree is the covenant of grace which God made with Israel. The natural branches are the nation of Israel who today are cut off. The grafted branches represent God's dealings with Christians in this present dispensation.

266. Romans 11:31 — Did God Reject Israel in Order to Save the Gentiles?

> Even so have these also now not believed, that through your mercy they also may obtain mercy (Romans 11:31).

In Romans 11 we have the state of Israel, the nation, which was set aside in order that the Gospel may go into all the world. Because Israel was in a sense the sacrifice which had to be paid for the Gospel going to the Gentiles, she is going to be restored in the millennium with great glory. If you will re-read the chapter carefully, you will notice that the restoration of Israel will be exceedingly glorious because they have suffered so much in their setting aside.

267. Does Romans 14:5-6 Teach That We Must Observe a Sabbath?

> One man esteemeth one day above another: another esteemeth every day alike. Let every man be fully persuaded in his own mind.
>
> He that regardeth the day, regardeth it unto the Lord; and he that regardeth not the day, to the Lord he doth not regard it (Romans 14:5-6).

The Christian has no sabbath. The Lord's day is not a command, but a privilege, and Romans 14:5-6 has to do with our liberty in Christ. The spirit, not the day, is of the greatest importance.

268. What Is the Meaning of the Phrase, "Saved by Fire," in I Corinthians 3:15?

"Saved; yet so as by fire" does not mean that the ones to whom this applies will lose their salvation, but that they shall not have rewards. "He himself shall be saved, yet so as by fire."

269. Does Marriage to a Believer Save a Sinner? In I Corinthians 7:14 It Is Said That the Unbeliever Is Sanctified by the Believing Wife. Please Explain.

> For the unbelieving husband is sanctified by the wife, and the unbelieving wife is sanctified by the husband: else were your children unclean; but now are they holy (I Cor. 7:14).

Concerning the matter of the sanctification of the husband, the passage is perfectly clear. The Word means that a husband is placed in a position of sanctification because he happens to be married to a believing wife, or vice versa. It does not mean that he is saved, but merely that it may be that through the testimony of the wife, the husband may be led to a knowledge of the Lord Jesus Christ. That is also the significance of the expression, "else were your children unholy." We believe that all babies who die before the age of accountability are saved through the finished work of the Lord Jesus Christ, and only as they grow up and reject the offer of salvation are they finally lost, so a baby is not saved because it is born in a Christian home and because it is baptized, but because of the completed work of the Lord Jesus Christ. Yet to be born in a Christian home places them in a position of peculiar privilege. This is the meaning of "holy" and "sanctification" in this verse.

This verse, therefore, does not refer to salvation at all, but rather to the position of privilege which the fellowship of a believer always brings.

270. Does Paul Discourage Marriage in I Corinthians 7:29?

> But this I say, brethren, the time is short: it remaineth, that both they that have wives be as though they had none (I Cor. 7:29).

In regard to this passage, you must remember that when Paul wrote this epistle, there was great persecution of the Christians and so Paul tells them that they should just "sit tight" for the present. Of course, we must take all these Scriptures in the light of the rest of revelation. Paul also teaches that he wants those who should, to marry and rear a family, while others who have been given a definite grace, may feel led of the Lord to remain single. We must remember that the Bible tells us that we shall all personally give an account of ourselves before God.

271. Please Explain I Corinthians 7:36.

This verse must be taken in its setting and connection with the rest of the chapter. It indicates here that Paul is teaching that when a man and woman have had relationships, it is their duty to become married. That is the responsibility and the Lord expects that, in order that they may be free from the sin of fornication.

272. Does the Bible Forbid Women to Bob the Hair? I Corinthians 11:6, 13-15.

> For if the woman be not covered, let her also be shorn: but if it be a shame for a woman to be shorn or shaven, let her be covered.
>
> Judge in yourselves: is it comely that a woman pray unto God uncovered?
>
> Doth not even nature itself teach you, that, if a man have long hair, it is a shame unto him?
>
> But if a woman have long hair, it is a glory to her: for her hair is given her for a covering (I Cor. 11:6, 13-15).

I am of the opinion that this has reference to a woman's hair. Although there are other interpretations, I know, I believe that the covering that Paul is referring to in the 6th verse refers definitely to a woman's glory, or her hair. This is definitely borne out in the 15th and 16th verses. Although Christian women everywhere have adopted the custom and habit of having their hair bobbed, I still believe that it is unscriptural and dishonoring to the Word of the Lord. I realize deeply how unpopular this teaching is, but we have to be faithful to the Word of God.

I do not mean to say, concerning children who have their hair cut, that there is anything wrong with this, but for mature Christian women who wish to be a testimony for the Lord Jesus Christ, I still believe that it hinders their testimony to have bobbed hair.

273. Which Is Most Important — the Death of Christ, or His Resurrection? I Corinthians 15:14-17

And if Christ be not risen, then is our preaching vain, and your faith is also vain.

Yea, and we are found false witnesses of God; because we have testified of God that he raised up Christ: whom he raised not up, if so be that the dead rise not.

For if the dead rise not, then is not Christ raised:

And if Christ be not raised, your faith is vain; ye are yet in your sins (I Cor. 15:14-17).

In regard to this passage, we must remember that the death and resurrection of Christ are inseparable. Without the resurrection of Christ, the death is sterile, and powerless; and without the death of Christ, the resurrection is an impossibility. If Christ had not risen, it would have been proof that He did not cancel every sin.

274. Please Explain I Corinthians 15:29, Being Baptized for the Dead.

Else what shall they do which are baptized for the dead, if the dead rise not at all? why are they then baptized for the dead? (I Cor. 15:29).

This passage in the original reads: "Else what shall they do which are now dead, who having been baptized, rise not at all?" The force here in this chapter in the original is, if there be no resurrection then those who have testified to their faith in Christ by baptism are dead without hope. You should read the verse entirely in the light of verse 19.

Baptism is our testimony of our relationship to Christ, and if there is no resurrection, then this hope is void.

275. Does Galatians 5:4 Teach That a Christian Can Be Lost?

> Christ is become of no effect unto you, whosoever of you are justified by the law; ye are fallen from grace (Gal. 5:4).

The entire context of the passage indicates that Paul is not speaking of falling away from salvation, but falling from grace. If you will read the entire verse, you will notice that he is talking about those that are trying to be justified by the law. Naturally anyone who is justified by the law is lost. The fourth verse, therefore, refers to people who had never been saved through simple faith in the Lord Jesus Christ. Notice the wording of verse 4: "whosoever of you are justified by the law; ye are fallen from grace." You will notice that he is speaking to those who seek justification through works instead of through faith. There were evidently those in the Galatian church who thought that they were not saved by grace alone, but had to add some law works to it. To refute this error, Paul writes this verse.

276. What Is Meant by God's Eternal Purpose in Ephesians 3:11?

> According to the eternal purpose which he purposed in Christ Jesus our Lord (Eph. 3:11).

This verse is one of the most precious in the entire epistle to the Ephesians, because it goes to the very root and the foundation of our redemption. You will notice that Paul in the 3rd of Ephesians is talking about the mystery of Israel's rejection during this present age, and the calling out of the Gentiles to be "fellow-heirs, and of the same body, and partakers of His promise in Christ by the gospel" (Verse 6). Then He tells us the purpose for calling out the Church, given in verse 9, "to make all men see what is the fellowship of the mystery," and that mystery, as you notice, was not revealed until after the Cross of Calvary. Then in verse 11 He gives us the foundation, "according to the eternal purpose." In other words, God always had in mind the setting aside of Israel and the bringing in of the Church age, and the calling of a Bride for His Son, the Lord Jesus Christ. So you see, our salvation does not depend upon anything that we do or have done, but upon His eternal purpose. This gives us security and peace and absolute assurance. As a result of that security and peace, we can take the 12th verse, "in whom we have boldness and access with confidence by the faith of Him." Will you notice that it it not by our faith, but *by the faith of Him.* It is the faith of the Lord Jesus Christ which He purposed even before the world was made which is the foundation of our redemption.

277. Should a Wife Always Obey Her Husband? Is This the Meaning of Ephesians 5:24?

Therefore as the church is subject unto Christ, so let the wives be to their own husbands in every thing (Eph. 5:24).

We must not take this verse by itself, but take the entire passage beginning at verse 21 to the end of the chapter, and we see that God's will is that husbands should follow the example of the Lord Jesus Christ in everything, and I am sure that a wife who has a husband like that would not find it difficult to be subject unto him. For a wife to be subject to an ungodly husband when it interferes with her worship of the Lord is, of course, not founded upon Scripture.

278. In Philippians 2:10-11 We Are Told That Every Knee Shall Bow Before Jesus. Does This Mean That All Will Ultimately Be Saved?

That at the name of Jesus every knee should bow, of things in heaven, and things in earth, and things under the earth;

>And that every tongue should confess that Jesus Christ
>is Lord, to the glory of God the Father (Phil. 2:10-11).

This has reference to the millennial age when all men
will be obedient to the Lord Jesus Christ. They will not
all be converted, but will obey Him through fear of punishment. That there will be those who are not truly converted is seen by the army which Satan is able to gather
at the end of the millennium according to Revelation
20:7-8.

279. Are We Commanded to Follow Preachers in All They Say? Is This the Meaning of Philippians 3:17?

>Brethren, be followers together of me, and mark them
>which walk so as ye have us for an ensample (Phil. 3:17).

In regard to your question concerning Philippians 3:17,
of course, Paul said, "Be ye followers of me," but before
any preacher can apply that verse to himself, he must be as
much an example as Paul himself was. There certainly is
nothing in the Bible to indicate that we are to follow any
preacher who is not walking according to the Word of God.
Of course, if a preacher sets an example in good things,
we ought to heed him, but always we are to take for
our example the Lord Jesus Christ and not a mere human
being.

280. Has the Gospel Ever Been Preached in All the World? Colossians 1:23 Seems to Imply This Clearly.

>If ye continue in the faith grounded and settled, and be
>not moved away from the hope of the gospel, which ye have
>heard, and which was preached to every creature which is
>under heaven; whereof I Paul am made a minister (Col.
>1:23).

In Colossians 1:23 Paul was stating that during his
lifetime the Gospel had been preached through all the
known world of his day. It certainly is sad that during
the years following, the Church has failed so miserably in
reaching all men with the Gospel.

281. Colossians 2:20:23 — Is There Any Foundation in the Bible for Different Denominations?

Wherefore if ye be dead with Christ from the rudiments of the world, why, as though living in the world, are ye subject to ordinances,

(Touch not; taste not; handle not;

Which all are to perish with the using;) after the commandments and doctrines of men?

Which things have indeed a shew of wisdom in will worship, and humility, and neglecting of the body; not in any honour to the satisfying of the flesh (Col. 2:20-23).

I am of the firm opinion that while there are many of God's faithful children in all denominations, that nevertheless sectarianism and denominationalism is sin. Much of the doctrine of present-day Protestantism is little more than a carry-over of medieval Catholicism. We recognize only One True Church, the Body of Christ, consisting of all born-again believers, no matter what their sectarian affiliation may be.

However, I am frank to state that whenever a denominational church fails to preach the full counsel of God, we ought to separate ourselves and worship God according to the dictates of our own conscience as prescribed in the Word of God, according to His way.

282. Who Is the AntiChrist? Please Explain II Thessalonians 2:1-3.

Now we beseech you, brethren, by the coming of our Lord Jesus Christ, and by our gathering together unto him,

That ye be not soon shaken in mind, or be troubled, neither by spirit, nor by word, nor by letter as from us, as that the day of Christ is at hand.

Let no man deceive you by any means: for that day shall not come, except there come a falling away first, and that man of sin be revealed, the son of perdition (II Thess. 2:1-3).

In this passage we are definitely assured that the antichrist will not be revealed until after the rapture of the

Church of Jesus Christ. Before the terrible tribulation
breaks upon the world, the Lord Jesus Christ will "descend
from heaven with a shout," according to I Thessalonians
4, and take out all of us believers and spare us from the
awful suffering of the tribulation period. This is called in
Scripture, "That Blessed Hope."

283. Does II Thessalonians 3:14-15 Teach That We Are to Refuse to Speak to An Erring Brother in Christ?

And if any man obey not our word by this epistle, note
that man, and have no company with him, that he may be
ashamed.

Yet count him not as an ememy, but admonish him as a
brother (II Thess. 3:14-15).

This has to do with a disobedient brother, and the
purpose of dis-fellowshipping him is that he may be
ashamed, and caused to repent and return again to the place
of obedience. I do not think that it means that we are not
to speak to them at all, because the next verse tells us
definitely, "yet count him not as an enemy, but admonish
him as a brother." The very fact that we are to admonish
him means that we are to speak to him. However, we are
not to endorse his actions or his conduct, whatever it may
be, but seek to bring him back to the place of fellowship
with the Lord.

284. I Timothy 2:15 — Please Explain the Phrase, "She Shall Be Saved in Childbearing."

Notwithstanding she shall be saved in childbearing, if
they continue in faith and charity and holiness with sobriety.

The scripture in Ist Timothy 2:15 is spoken concerning
Eve, as verse 14 clearly shows, where salvation depended
upon her giving birth to a child through which the seed of
the woman, the Redeemer, Jesus Christ, was to be born.
In order for Eve and the rest to be saved, a kinsman redeemer must be provided, and this could only be done

through Eve giving birth to a son. It has nothing to do with salvation through bearing children today.

285. I Timothy 5:9 —Should Widows Be Admitted into the Local Church?

Let not a widow be taken into the number under three-score years old, having been the wife of one man.

Concerning I Timothy 5:9, this chapter deals with the support of poor widows in the assembly. You will notice the verse preceding I Tim. 5:9 instructs the Church to not support these widows if they have relatives who are able to support them. The ninth verse, therefore, has to do not only with admitting widows under 60 years into the assembly, but especially supporting them because, as verse 11 indicates, they may again marry and even an unbeliever has the benefit of the support which the Christians have given them. I believe the real lesson is that we ought to care for our own loved ones when they are in need, and not to burden the Church with it.

286. Does II Timothy 2:4 Sanction War by Believers?

No man that warreth entangleth himself with the affairs of this life; that he may please him who hath chosen him to be a soldier (II Tim. 2:4).

This passage has to do with the ministry, and the spiritual warfare of ministers, and they are admonished not to be engrossed with material things so that they cannot give all of their attention to the work of the ministry.

287. What Is Meant in II Timothy 2:20-22 by Vessels Unto Honor and Vessels Unto Dishonor?

But in a great house there are not only vessels of gold and of silver, but also of wood and of earth; and some to honour, and some to dishonour.

If a man therefore purge himself from these, he shall be a vessel unto honour, sanctified, and meet for the master's use, and prepared unto every good work.

Flee also youthful lusts: but follow righteousness, faith, charity, peace, with them that call on the Lord out of a pure heart (II Tim. 2:20-22).

I believe that the "vessels" here represent two kinds of believers — those who are carnal, and those who are spiritual; those who bring reproach upon the cause of Christ, and those who are a real testimony and a real witness for the cause of Christ. Of course, these things are going to be taken care of at the judgment seat of Christ, and it is not our business to judge while we are here. We must leave that judgment entirely in the hands of the Lord.

288. Titus 2:14 — What Is Meant by "Peculiar People" Found in This Verse and Also in I Peter 2:9?

Who gave himself for us, that he might redeem us from all iniquity, and purify unto himself a peculiar people, zealous of good works (Titus 2:14).

But ye are a chosen generation, a royal priesthood, an holy nation, a peculiar people (I Peter 2:9).

In regard to the word, "peculiar," it comes from the word, "peculium" which means "a very precious possession which belonged to the individual alone, and was never to be sold or disposed of." This is the meaning in the Scriptures. We are the "peculiar" possession of the Lord Jesus Christ which He purchased with His own blood, and will never let us go. It does not mean we are to be "peculiar" in speech, dress or action.

289. Does Hebrews 3:6 Teach That a Believer Can Lose His Eternal Security?

But Christ as a son over his own house; whose house are we, if we hold fast the confidence and the rejoicing of the hope firm unto the end (Hebrews 3:6).

Concerning your question, I take it that your friend is having difficulty with the part that says, "if we hold fast the confidence and the rejoicing of the hope firm unto the end." You must remember that this is not a matter of salvation, but he is talking about confidence and rejoicing and hope. This is quite a different matter than salvation. The illustration which the writer of Hebrews is using is that of the children of Israel who were out of Egypt, but did not reach Canaan, but died in the wilderness. They were still children of Israel, even though they did not reach the final Canaan shore. Canaan is not heaven, but represents "victory," and these represent Christians who, while they are out of Egypt and saved, never attain to the highest purpose for which God has called them. Of course, it is always dangerous to hang any truth on one particular verse. We must take the whole body of Scripture, and the rest of Scripture is so clear in regard to the fact of eternal life and eternal security, that even though we cannot understand every single verse, we are not to reject a truth because one verse seems to contradict it.

290. Does Hebrews 5:9 Teach That Jesus Was Not Perfect?

And being made perfect, he became the author of eternal salvation unto all them that obey him (Hebrews 5:9).

It must be remembered that while Jesus was perfect God and also perfect Man, that as a Saviour He could not be perfect without meeting the demands of God and making Himself a sacrifice that sinners might live. The word, "perfect," refers here not to His character or His perfection, but His work. Obedience, of course, depends upon faith. Unless a man has faith, he cannot obey. Salvation is obeying God's command, "Believe on the Lord Jesus Christ, and thou shalt be saved."

291. Does Hebrews 6 Refer to Believers or Professors Only?

Hebrews 6 was written to Christians and warns believers against living in wilful sin. It does not mean that a Christian can be lost, but rather, that God will judge his sin. Once a Christian has eternal life, he can never lose it.

Hebrews 6 and 10 are both warnings to saved believers against sin, lest God's judgment should rest upon them. This, however, has nothing to do with salvation. These chapters do not deal with losing salvation, nor with the unregenerate, but have to do with Christians who depart from their first love and lose their rewards, *not* their salvation.

292. What Is the Meaning of Hebrews 6:1-2?

Therefore leaving the principles of the doctrine of Christ, let us go on unto perfection; not laying again the foundation of repentance from dead works, and of faith toward God,

Of the doctrine of baptisms, and of laying on of hands, and of resurrection of the dead, and of eternal judgment (Hebrews 6:1-2).

In regard to Hebrews 6:1-2, there are some who try to make us believe that we must leave behind repentance, and faith, and baptism, etc. However, this is not the meaning. The writer of Hebrews is talking about Christian growth, and while we continue in the faith and repentance and all the others, we are not to remain by these elementary doctrines, but to go on to the deeper things of God, or as the writer puts it, "let us go on unto perfection." If this text means that we are to lay aside these things, then we overthrow the resurrection and eternal judgment and all the fundamental truths. These fundamental truths must be believed by us, and then we are to go on into the further knowledge of the Word of God.

293. Please Explain Hebrews 11:37-40.

They were stoned, they were sawn asunder, were tempted, were slain with the sword: they wandered about in sheepskins and goatskins; being destitute, afflicted, tormented;

(Of whom the world was not worthy:) they wandered in deserts, and in mountains, and in dens and caves of the earth.

And these all, having obtained a good report through
faith, received not the promise:
God having provided some better thing for us, that
they without us should not be made perfect (Hebrews
11:37-40).

This refers to the fact that the Old Testament saints who
suffered and died for the sake of their testimony will not
be resurrected and raised until the Church is complete.
"They have not yet received the promise" means they have
not yet received the reward, but that better things will be
shared by them when we as the body of Christ are raptured
at the coming of the Lord. The Old Testament saints will
not be raised until the body of Christ in this dispensation
has been completed.

294. Please Explain Hebrews 12:14, with Special Reference to Holiness.

Follow peace with all men, and holiness, without which
no man shall see the Lord (Hebrews 12:14).

Concerning this passage, you must remember that holiness
and sanctification are used in three different senses throughout the Bible. *First of all*, sanctification and holiness can
refer to objects, such as a tabernacle, or even a day. The
Lord says, for instance, concerning the sabbath day,
"therefore, the Lord sanctified the sabbath day." This
means that He set it apart from other days as being unique
and distinct in its purpose.

The *second* meaning of sanctification or holiness is that
certain persons are set aside for certain work. The priests
of the Old Testament were sanctified for their service, and
we as children of God are also said to have been sanctified. This is our position in Christ.

The *third* meaning of sanctification is practical, which
means a growth in grace, and Christ-likeness during all
the days of our life, until we become like Him when we
shall see Him. I hope that this answers your question. A

great deal of harm has been done by a misunderstanding concerning the simple teaching of the Word of God in regard to this matter.

295. Why Is It Said in Hebrews 13:12-13 That Jesus "Suffered Outside the Gate?"

> Wherefore Jesus also, that he might sanctify the people with his own blood, suffered without the gate.
> Let us go forth therefore unto him without the camp, bearing his reproach (Hebrews 13:12-13).

Your question on Hebrews 13:12-13 refers to the fact that the Lord Jesus Christ was crucified outside of the gates of Jerusalem. His own people had rejected the King, and therefore, took Him outside the kingly city, and it speaks of His rejection for the sake and the cause of the will of God. Now, He is our example, and we too should be willing to separate ourselves from all apostate religions and from all false doctrines, and walk alone, if need be, outside the camp of organized religion if this becomes necessary.

Verse 13 of this passage is an admonition to Christians to walk the separated life. Jesus said while He was here, "If they have hated Me, they will hate you," and "if any man will be my disciple, let him deny himself, take up his cross, and follow Me." As followers of the Lord Jesus Christ, we must be willing to leave the camp of the world, and the unbelievers, and even false religious professors, and be willing to walk alone with Christ in the path of separation.

296. James 5:14 — What Is the Difference Between Healing in the Name of Jesus, and Healing in the Name of the Lord?

> Is any sick among you? let him call for the elders of the church; and let them pray over him, anointing him with oil in the name of the Lord (James 5:14).

In regard to your question concerning James 5:14 and

divine healing, I suggest that you read I Corinthians 12, verse 3, where Paul tells us that "no man can call Jesus Lord except by the Spirit of God." The evidence of the spirit of God in a movement is that we acknowledge the Lordship of the Lord Jesus Christ. You will probably observe that in many, many meetings which are unscriptural, the name of "Jesus" is constantly used without the name, "Lord." We are not only to accept Christ as our Saviour, but He is also to become the Lord of our life. James is not speaking about public healing meetings, but calling the elders of the church to go to the sick one.

297. James 5:15 Is Used by Modern Divine(?) Healers to Substantiate Their Claims. Just What Is James Talking About?

And the prayer of faith shall save the sick, and the Lord shall raise him up; and if he have committed sins, they shall be forgiven him (James 5:15).

In regard to the matter of James 5, the word for "save" in the 15th verse means to "save from the sickness" with which the party mentioned in this chapter was afflicted. This healing is for today, but not for promiscuous healing. It refers, as the context definitely indicates, to only those cases of sickness which are caused by unconfessed sin in the life of the believer. These sins are the result of failure to judge our own iniquity according to I Corinthians 11. It is only for believers who are living in unconfessed sin. These cannot be healed until first they are saved from their sin, and confess it before the Lord. In this same connection, James 5:20 —

Let him know, that he which converteth the sinner from the error of his way shall save a soul from death, and shall hide a multitude of sins.

This has to do with bodily healing, on the condition of repentance and faith and confession of sin. If you will read the preceding verses in this fifth chapter, you will notice that the apostle is speaking concerning the healing of bodies in reply to the prayer of faith. It is, therefore, quite clear that James is speaking in the twentieth verse about physical death and not spiritual death at all. It comes under the same heading as I Corinthians 11, where the Lord sometimes visits His children with physical death if they refuse to repent and confess their sins. Certainly we cannot apply this to spiritual death.

298. Who Are the "Spirits in Prison" to Whom Jesus Is Said to Have Preached in I Peter 3:19-20?

By which also he went and preached unto the spirits in prison;

Which sometime were disobedient, when once the long-suffering of God waited in the days of Noah, while the ark was a preparing, wherein few, that is, eight souls were saved by water.

The statement is that "Christ preached to the spirits in prison which sometimes were disobedient"; that is, they were disobedient sinners, like all of us, but were saved by the grace of God. In the twentieth verse of the third chapter of First Peter, the word, "once" is not in the original, and it should read as follows: "Which sometimes were disobedient when the longsuffering of God waited in the days of Noah." That is, these people, like all sinners, were disobedient, but God's longsuffering waited in order to give them an opportunity to repent and be saved. They represent, therefore, the saints of the Old Testament who, while they were sinners, were saved by faith in the Lord Jesus Christ. In this connection one should read Titus 3:3, where we are told concerning ourselves, "For we ourselves also were sometimes foolish, disobedient, deceived, serving divers lusts and pleasures, living in malice and envy, hateful, and hating one another." All of us were disobedient — in fact, Christ came to save disobedient sinners. I hope that this will be of some help to you. Of course, this pas-

sage in I Peter must be read in the light of the other passages mentioned in the Scriptures.

299. Does I Peter 4:8 Teach That We Can Save Sinners?

And above all things have fervent charity among yourselves: for charity shall cover the multitude of sins (I Peter
4:8).

I Peter 4:8 has nothing to do with the forgiveness of
sins. The writer is speaking about covering a multitude of
sins, as far as the eyes of people is concerned. Peter is
speaking of love, and if we really love our brethren, we
will not expose their sins, and gossip about them, but
rather, we will try to protect them and defend them, and to
cover up their faults, rather than to advertize them before
the world. This is the meaning of this passage, and has
nothing to do whatsoever with the forgiveness of sins by
the Lord Himself.

300. Does II Peter 2:1 Teach That a Believer Can Go to Hell?

But there were false prophets also among the people,
even as there shall be false teachers among you, who
privily shall bring in damnable heresies, even denying the
Lord that bought them and bring upon themselves swift
destruction (II Peter 2:1).

I have always felt that these people in II Peter 2:1
were not saved, who had only made a profession, and then
had gone back on that profession. I do not believe that
they ever knew the Lord Jesus Christ in reality. This passage has been called into question by many theologians,
but this is my personal opinion.

The same is true also of II Peter 2:19-22:

While they promise them liberty, they themselves are the
servants of corruption: for of whom a man is overcome,
of the same is he brought in bondage.

For if after they have escaped the pollutions of the world
through the knowledge of the Lord and Saviour Jesus

Christ, they are again entangled therein, and overcome, the latter end is worse with them than the beginning.

For it had been better for them not to have known the way of righteousness, than, after they have known it, to turn from the holy commandment delivered unto them.

But it is happened unto them according to the true proverb, The dog is turned to his own vomit again; and the sow that was washed to her wallowing in the mire (II Peter 2:19-22).

Peter is speaking here as he does in the balance of the chapter about false teachers and false prophets, who make a profession of knowing Christ, but have never been born again, and have not been truly saved. They have made outward profession, as the verse will show, but they have left even that profession and gone back again into the life of sin which they had apparently renounced. This to me is the meaning of these verses and describes for us the apostasy of the last days.

301. I John 1:9 — Will God Forgive Our Sins If We Fail to Make Restitution?

If we confess our sins, he is faithful and just to forgive us our sins, and to cleanse us from all unrighteousness (I John 1:9).

Wherever possible the Lord expects that we shall not only confess our sins, but also seek to make right the wrong, but where this is impossible, the Lord forgives and I John 1:9 covers all sins which are confessed to the Lord. I would not worry about the incident at all if you have done all you could and have confessed it to Him.

302. Is "Sinless Perfection" Taught in I John 3:9?

Whosoever is born of God doth not commit sin; for his seed remaineth in him: and he cannot sin, because he is born of God (I John 3:9).

We must first of all remember that John is speaking about two natures. In this particular chapter, when he says,

"If we confess our sins, He is faithful and just to forgive us our sins," he is speaking of the fact that the old nature does sin. He says, for instance, "If we say we have no sin, we deceive ourselves." That is the first thing to remember, that the old nature which is still in us is always trying to sin and can sin.

Then, when he speaks about him that is born of God not committing sin, he is talking about the new nature. Now, both of these things are true. While the old nature is sinful, and always will continue to be so until we are relieved from it at death or the coming of the Lord, it is also true that the new nature, that is, the divine nature, born of God, cannot and never does sin. This brings about the struggle in the Christian life, so that Paul could say, "the flesh lusteth against the spirit, and the spirit lusteth against the flesh, so that we cannot do things that we would." Our victory, therefore, becomes the victory of the new nature over the old.

303. The Jehovah's Witnesses Have Been Calling on Me, and I Am Wondering How I Should Treat Them? I John 5:7

For there are three that bear record in heaven, the Father, the Word, and the Holy Ghost: and these three are one (I John 5:7).

I have found in my past experience that it is little use to talk or deal with these Russelites. They are all on one single line of thought, and are usually looking for an argument. My worst and most serious objection to Russelism or to Jehovah's Witnesses, or the Watch Tower people, by whatever name they may be called, is that they are always trying to upset and disturb people who are already believers, while they seem to make absolutely no effort whatsoever to win the unsaved for Christ. This alone brands it as an error and an "ism." It is a dangerous doctrine, and if I were you, I would not allow them to sway me or

influence me in any way by their one-sided doctrine. Since
they do not believe in the blood as we do, and do not
believe in the eternal, pre-existent deity of the Lord Jesus
Christ, we cannot accept any of their doctrine.

304. Is It True That I John 5:7-8 Is Not Contained in Any Greek Manuscript Which Was Written Earlier Than the Fifth Century?

Since we are not in possession today of the original
manuscript, but the earliest manuscript of the New Testament which we have is dated quite some time after the
first century, there is a variation in the different manuscripts, and some of them have omitted certain passages,
among which are I John 5:7-8. However, it does appear
in many of the other manuscripts, and so I believe that it
was a part of the original.

305. Revelation — A Brief Outline of the Book

The first three verses of Revelation 4 give us a picture of
the Rapture of the Church of Jesus Christ at the end of
this dispensation. Chapter 1 is a picture of the glory of
Christ in His second coming. Chapter 2 and 3 give us
the history of the Church from Pentecost to the rapture.
The seven churches are seven definite stages of church
history, Ephesus being the apostolic church, and Laodicea
being the age in which we now live.

After the Lord Jesus Christ has been pushed out of the
church as we see in Laodicea at the end of chapter 3,
it is time for the Lord to return. So, while John was
looking into heaven, the heavens were opened, and the voice
called him to come up. John represents the church, and as
soon as he is called away, he has a vision of the glory of
Christ in heaven as seen in the remainder of Chapter 4,
and all of Chapter 5. Then follows the tribulation period,
chapters 6 to 19. At the end of the tribulation the Lord

Jesus comes back *with* His Church, as found in the last part of that chapter.

306. Revelation 1:4 — The Seven Spirits

John to the seven churches which are in Asia: Grace be unto you, and peace, from him which is, and which was, and which is to come; and from the seven Spirits which are before his throne (Rev. 1:4).

In regard to the seven spirits of God, you must remember that there is only one Holy Spirit, but this spirit has seven manifestations, or activities. These seven spirits, therefore, refer to the activities of the one Holy Spirit, and not the seven separate spirits.

The Bible does not tell us just exactly what these seven spirits of God are. In Isaiah 11, verse 2, however, we are told what they represent, and we are there informed it is the spirit of wisdom and understanding, of counsel and of might, of knowledge and of the fear of the Lord.

307. Revelation 2 and 3 — The Seven Churches

In regard to your question concerning Revelation 2 and 3, the fact that John says that this is a prophecy indicates definitely that this was still in the future when John was writing. The seven churches in Asia Minor represent the seven distinct stages of church development in its nominal sense. I realize the fact that there undoubtedly were these seven historical churches to which John actually wrote, but that does not mean that they could not also have a prophetic meaning. We have many instances of this in the Bible.

For instance, the fig tree in Matthew 21 and Mark 11 was an actual fig tree which Jesus cursed, but we also know that it represented the nation of Israel and their future. Maybe I can illustrate what I mean in this way. Suppose you have a lock that you would like to open. You have a bunch of one hundred keys, and find that one single key fits the lock exactly. Then you know, even though the key may not be marked in any way, that that is the key which was meant for that particular lock. In the same way, the interpretation of the seven churches in Asia fits exactly the lock of the history of the church from Pentecost until now.

308. What Are the Meanings of the Names of the Seven Churches Mentioned in Revelation, Chapters 2 and 3?

The Seven Churches in Revelation, and their meanings are listed as follows:
1. Ephesus — Desired One
2. Smyrna — Crushed or Persecuted One
3. Pergamos — Married One
4. Thyatira — Continual Sacrifice
5. Sardis — "That which remaineth," or Remnant
6. Philadelphia — Brotherly Love
7. Laodicea — Nauseating or Lukewarm One

309. In Revelation 2:5 We Are Told to Repent and Do Our First Works. What Are These?

Remember therefore from whence thou art fallen, and repent, and do the first works (Rev. 2:5).

In regard to your question on repenting and doing the first works, this was written to the Church but also has a personal application, and means just what it says. They had departed from their first love, and the Lord urges them to repent of their sins and to go back to that first period of fruitfulness after their conversion.

310. Who Are the Overcomers in Revelation 2:17?

He that hath an ear, let him hear what the Spirit saith unto the churches; To him that overcometh will I give to eat of the hidden manna, and will give him a white stone, and in the stone a new name written, which no man knoweth saving he that receiveth it (Rev. 2:17).

This refers, of course, to the reward of the believer when Christ comes. We *believe* to be saved, but there is also a crown and a reward for those who overcome, which is on the basis of our faithfulness and works.

311. Can You Tell Me From Scripture Where Heaven Is?

I am sorry that I cannot tell you exactly "where" heaven is. Some theologians claim it is in the "empty place" in the north. Astronomers tell us there is an empty area in the northern heavens where no planets or stars are visible. On this fact, and the references in Job 26:7 and Psalm 75:6, many believe that heaven is located somewhere in the region of this empty place.

312. Was Jesus A Created Being? I Have Been Told This Is Taught In Revelation 3:14.

> And unto the angel of the church of the Laodiceans write; These things saith the Amen, the faithful and true witness, the beginning of the creation of God (Rev. 3:14).

Concerning the statement in Revelation 3:14 about Jesus being the beginning of the creation of God, this verse must be taken, of course, with the rest of the Bible which definitely teaches that Christ is not created, but that He always was. For instance, John 1:1-3 definitely states that Jesus is the Creator, and therefore, He existed from eternity before the creation. The passage in Revelation 3:14, therefore, does not mean that Jesus was the first creature, but rather that He is the One who began the creation; that is, that He Himself is the Creator.

313. How Can Jesus and His Father Sit on the Same Throne, As in Revelation 3:21?

> To him that overcometh will I grant to sit with me in my throne, even as I also overcame, and am set down with my Father in his throne (Rev. 3:21).

Your question concerning Christ and Jehovah both sitting

on the Throne will be completely answered, I am sure, if you will read Revelation 3:21. Christ sits on His Father's throne. In chapter four Christ is pictured on the Throne. In chapter five, it is the Father.

314. What Is the Meaning of the Four Beasts in Revelation 4:7?

> And the first beast was like a lion, and the second beast like a calf, and the third beast had a face as a man, and the fourth beast was like a flying eagle (Rev. 4:7).

The four beasts in Revelation chapter four may be taken as representing the Gospel in heaven, corresponding to the four-fold work of the Lord Jesus Christ as recorded in the four gospel records. In *Matthew* we have the *Lion;* in *Mark* we have the *Ox;* in *Luke* the *Man;* and in *John* we have the *Eagle.* It is the full testimony concerning Christ.

315. Please Explain the Twenty-Four Elders in Revelation 4:4.

> And round about the throne were four and twenty seats: and upon the seats I saw four and twenty elders sitting, clothed in white raiment; and they had on their heads crowns of gold (Rev. 4:4).

The twenty-four elders in Revelation 4 are the representatives of both the Old Testament and the New Testament saints; the saved before the Cross, and the saved after the Cross. As there were twelve apostles, as well as twelve tribes, the twenty-four represent all of these. Elders in Scripture are always the representatives of the congregation.

316. Revelation 6 — the Seals in Revelation

The first seal in Revelation 6 is the beginning of the antichrist's reign, and represents a false peace, to be followed by war in the second seal, when we read that peace shall be taken from the earth. The white horse is the imitation of the true Christ.

The opening of the seals by Christ is the loosing of the judgments on earth in the first half of the tribulation.

317. Who Are the 144,000 of Revelation 7?

The servants are the 144,000 Jews which are mentioned in the rest of this chapter. The Lord will not permit the judgment of God to fall on the earth until they are given a safe place so they will not be destroyed in the judgments to follow. "Seal" in Scriptures is always the Holy Spirit. The people are supernaturally protected, and the 144,000 are not Gentiles or Christians, but definitely Jews, as verses 4 to 8 indicate.

318. Who Are the Multitude without Number in Revelation 7:4-8 Who Are Saved in the Tribulation?

In Revelation 7:4-8 we have the conversion of the remnant of Israel during the tribulation, 144,000 in number. After their conversion, they preach the Gospel to the nations who have not yet heard it, and as a result of the preaching of these 144,000 Israelites, a great company of people from all nations are saved, but are martyred for their faith, and will be resurrected at the Second Coming of Christ after the tribulation. You, of course, understand that the Church is taken out before the tribulation, and this company in Revelation 7:9 are tribulation saints. They are the same ones you will find described in Revelation 20:4.

319. Please Give Me Light on Revelation 9:3.

> And there came out of the smoke locusts upon the earth: and unto them was given power, as the scorpions of the earth have power (Rev. 9:3).

It is true that they were commanded not to hurt those which had the seal of God in their foreheads, but it does not say that Satan commanded this, but from verse 4 we imply that God sent forth the command that they were *not* to hurt His own children. You will notice that it says all through the passage "it was commanded thee," or "to them it was given" implying that while Satan is on the loose, God is still keeping His hand on the affairs of men, and will not permit the devil to go any farther than God pleases.

320. What Nations Are Referred to in Revelation 9:16?

> And the number of the army of the horsemen were two hundred thousand thousand: and I heard the number of them (Rev. 9:16).

I do not believe that this passage refers specifically either to the Russian army or the United Nations armies, but this is a supernatural army which comes up from the pit. Just who they will be, we do not know, but it does seem that it will consist of an army of possibly demons, and not human beings, here upon the earth.

Personally, I do not believe that it ties in with Ezekiel 39, although it will occur at approximately the same time. There are many of these matters which are not fully clear, but as the prophecies are fulfilled, and the Scriptures unfold, we begin to get more and more light on some of these matters. For this reason we have to leave some of these unanswered, until we have more light on it.

321. Who Are the Two Witnesses of Revelation 11?

I believe Moses and Elijah to be the two witnesses because in the 11th chapter of Revelation, the particular wonders and miracles ascribed to the two witnesses were those which Moses and Elijah performed. For instance, shutting up heaven for three and one-half years, and causing fire to come down from heaven, are miracles which point to Elijah. Turning water into blood and smiting the earth with plagues are what Moses did.

Moreover, the last chapter of Malachi tells us that Elijah
will return. Also in the 17th chapter of Matthew, it was
Moses and Elijah who were with Christ on the Mount,
and finally, the testimony of these two alone would be
believed by the Jews, since Moses was the one who led them
out of physical bondage, and Elijah was the one who led
them out of spiritual bondage. This is the ministry of the
two witnesses in Revelation 11.

322. If the Last Trump Occurs at the Rapture (I Cor. 15:52), What About the Trumpets in Revelation 11?

I am quite familiar with the teaching of the mid-tribula-
tion rapture. However, if you will remember that there are
two last trumps, one for the saved, and the other for the
unsaved, I think it will clear up your difficulty. The "last
trump" in I Corinthians 15 is for the Church. The "last
trump" in Revelation 11 is for the wicked on the earth.
The first is the trumpet of redemption, and the second the
trumpet of judgment.

323. How Long Will the Great Tribulation Last? Revelation 11:3

> And I will give power unto my two witnesses, and they
> shall prophesy a thousand two hundred and threescore days,
> clothed in sackcloth (Rev. 11:3).

In regard to your question concerning Revelation 11, the
three and one-half years or forty-two months is the last
half of the tribulation period. It corresponds to the last
half of Daniel's seventieth week. The tribulation will last
for seven years, and from the appearance of the antichrist
on the scene and the witnesses in Revelation 11, it will be
just forty-two months until the return of the Lord.

324. What Is Meant by the Rewards in Revelation 11:18?

> And the nations were angry, and thy wrath is come, and
> the time of the dead, that they should be judged, and that

> thou shouldest give reward unto thy servants the prophets, and to the saints, and them that fear thy name, small and great; and shouldest destroy them which destroy the earth (Rev. 11:18).

This has to do with the giving of rewards at the end of the tribulation period. There are no unbelieving dead mentioned in this verse. Remember, the judgment seat of Christ begins at the Rapture, but the rewards are not given out until after the tribulation period and at the beginning of the millennium. (See especially Revelation 19:7-9). Of course, this is also the time when God judges the wicked at the Battle of Armageddon.

325. Please Explain the Meaning of "The Cup" in Revelation 14:8-10.

> And there followed another angel, saying, Babylon is fallen, is fallen, that great city, because she made all nations drink of the wine of the wrath of her fornication.
> And the third angel followed them, saying with a loud voice, If any man worship the beast and his image, and receive his mark in his forehead, or in his hand,
> The same shall drink of the wine of the wrath of God, which is poured out without mixture into the cup of his indignation; and he shall be tormented with fire and brimstone in the presence of the holy angels, and in the presence of the Lamb (Rev. 14:8-10).

In regard to your question concerning Revelation 14:8-10, "the wine of the wrath" speaks of the judgment of Almighty God. The "cup" in Scripture is used both for salvation and for wrath. Jesus drank the "cup" of God's wrath for us in the Garden. To those who refuse His sacrifice they will have to drink of the cup of God's wrath themselves.

326. What Is the Meaning of "That Great City" in Revelation 17:18?

> And the woman which thou sawest is that great city, which reigneth over the kings of the earth (Rev. 17:18).

Concerning "that great city" in Revelation 17:18, there is no question in my mind that it refers to the city of Rome, especially in its religious aspect. The 17th and 18th chapters of Revelation are a clear picture of the Roman Catholic Church in the latter days. It is easy to understand these things now, in view of the things which are happening. The aggressiveness of the Catholic Church in the last few years, together with their recent celebration, and their new doctrine of the rapture of the Queen of Heaven, the Virgin Mary, together with the so-called visions of the Pope, and now the attempt of our President to appoint an ambassador to the Vatican at Rome, are all indications that we are rapidly approaching the fulfillment of Revelation 17 and 18. However, we believe with all our hearts that before this happens, the Lord Jesus Christ is going to return. How near it must be!

327. Where Do All the People in the Vast Armies Described in Revelation 19 Come From if the Wicked Are Destroyed in the Tribulation?

Your question concerning Revelation 19 refers to the children who will be born during the millennial age, both Jews and Gentiles. These children will have to be born again even as others. Those who are saved will never die, and since the Bible tells us that life will be greatly increased, and the people will live to be 1,000 years old, the population will mount swiftly. This accounts for the fact that at the end of the millennium there will be a great multitude even of the unsaved to join Satan when he is let loose for a little season.

328. What Is the "Testimony of Jesus" in Revelation 19:10?

And I fell at his feet to worship him. And he said unto me, See thou do it not: I am thy fellowservant, and of thy brethren that have the testimony of Jesus: worship God: for the testimony of Jesus is the spirit of prophecy (Rev. 19:10).

In regard to the quotation in Revelation 19:10, this refers entirely to the fact that Christ is the center and circumference of all prophecy. The entire Bible from beginning to end speaks directly or indirectly of the Lord Jesus Christ, and the Spirit's work is to take the things of Christ, and to show them unto us. This, I believe, is the connection in which it is used here.

I am fully aware that this is being used by some cults in a different way, but we can not stretch it beyond its meaning. It means simply this, that if we are to enter into the spirit of prophecy of these last days, it will only be as we keep Christ in the center, and recognize that His coming is the culmination of all prophecy as given to us by the Spirit.

329. What Happens to the Wicked at Jesus' Coming? Revelation 19:21

And the remnant were slain with the sword of him that sat upon the horse, which sword proceeded out of his mouth: and all the fowls were filled with their flesh (Rev. 19:21).

The "remnant" in this verse are those who have received the mark of the beast and have followed the antichrist. These will be slain at the end of the tribulation, while the ones who have not received the mark of the beast will go into the Millennial Kingdom and form the nations during the reign of Christ.

330. Revelation 21:24 — Who Are the Nations Who Enter the Kingdom?

And the nations of them which are saved shall walk in the light of it: and the kings of the earth do bring their glory and honour into it (Rev. 21:24).

We must understand these nations as composed of individuals. God does not save entire nations, although He does bless them in a national sense, but salvation must always be individual.

Then in regard to your question concerning anyone being saved after the rapture, those who have heard the Gospel and rejected it will not have another opportunity, but only those who have never heard the Gospel will have opportunity, according to Revelation 7, to receive the Lord Jesus Christ as Saviour.

331. Can Our Names Be Erased From the Book of Life? Some Say That Revelation 22:19 Teaches This.

And if any man shall take away from the words of the book of this prophecy, God shall take away his part out of the book of life, and out of the holy city, and from the things which are written in this book (Rev. 22:19).

The passage in Revelation 22:19 has always been a difficult one, and good Bible students are not at all in accord on the matter of its interpretation. There are those who tell us that all people are written in the Book of Life at birth, and when they come to years of accountability and reject the Lord, that their name is taken out. Still others tell us that God knew from eternity who would be in the Book of Life, and also who would reject the Gospel, and was able to take out their names from the beginning. It is not an easy passage to interpret, and we have to leave some of these things for eternity, where we shall know as we are known.

CHAPTER 12

DOCTRINE AND THEOLOGY

332. What Is the Difference Between Law and Grace?

The Bible plainly teaches that those under the law are
under the curse, and they are not justified in God's sight.
If there is anything of our works to earn salvation, it is
not of grace, and if it is not of grace, we cannot be saved.
Read carefully the following references: Romans 3:20, 28;
Romans 4:5; Romans 7:1-4; Galatians 2:19-21; Galatians
3:10 and 13.

333. How Do You Explain the Trinity?

The Trinity, that is, three persons in one, is a mystery
which is revealed in the Bible, but cannot be understood
by the human mind. Since man is finite, and God is infinite,
this is one of those things which must be accepted by faith,
even though it cannot be reasoned out. The Trinity cannot be explained but it must be believed because the
Bible teaches it throughout.

334. What Is the Difference Between the Justification of the Sinner and the Justification of the Saint?

Paul, in Romans, speaks of the justification of the
sinner, *in the sight of God*. James speaks of the justification of a saint, *in the sight of men*. Sinners are justified
by faith before God but our faith cannot be proven before
men except by our works. God can see our faith, but men
can only see our works.

335. According to John 20:23, Can Man Forgive Sins?

In regard to your problem concerning this passage of Scripture, remember that this was not spoken to any one individual, but to the apostles, and to all of us who preach the story of grace. Whenever we preach, we are "a savor of life, or a savor of death." If men believe the Gospel, their sins are remitted by the Lord. If they reject it, their sins are retained. None can forgive sins, but God alone.

336. Does the Bible Teach the Doctrine of Election, and Can You Help Me to Understand It?

In regard to "election," and especially Romans 9:22, we are dealing with the relationship of our faith and free will against the sovereign and elective purpose of Almighty God. That there is divine, sovereign election in Scripture cannot be denied. According to Ephesians 1:4-5, we are saved from before the foundation of the world. According to I Peter 1:2, we are elect according to the foreknowledge of God. For this reason, all the saved are elected to go to heaven, while God who foreknew those who would reject Him, permits the unsaved to be lost forever.

It is a knotty problem, and yet we must believe that God does all things right. The free will of man and the sovereign grace of God do not seem to harmonize in our reasoning, but God is infinite and wise. Since He reveals it, we believe it, even though we cannot understand it. We must read Romans 9 in the light of John 3.

337. What Is "Unconfessed Sin?"

Unconfessed sin, in Scripture, is continually practicing sins which we know are contrary to the Word of God. It is not only necessary to confess our sins, but to forsake them as well. When we are willing to do this, the Lord forgives and cleanses us according to I John 1:9, "If we confess our sins, he is faithful and just to forgive us our sins, and to cleanse us from all unrighteousness."

338. Should Our Sins Be Confessed to the Presiding Elder of the Church?

The Bible teaches us that we are to confess our *sins* to God, and our *faults* one to another, and not necessarily to the whole world. We are definitely told in Scripture not to judge one another. (See I Corinthians 4:5.) I believe that much of this confession is a remnant of Catholicism.

339. Should the Sins of Believers Be Confessed Publicly or Privately?

A good rule which I advise people to follow is that private sins call for private confession to the Lord, and to the Lord only. In the case of public sins, however, I believe that they should be publicly confessed.

340. Please Explain to Me the Difference Between the Sin Unto Death, the Sin Against the Holy Ghost, and the Unpardonable Sin.

The "sin unto death" is sin committed by Christians resulting in judgment, but not in the loss of salvation. They are sins deliberately practiced in spite of full knowledge of their presence. Such sins may result in death. (See 1 Cor. 11:28-32.)

The "sin against the Holy Ghost" was a national sin, committed by Israel, while Jesus was on earth, and finally in the rejection of the Holy Spirit at Stephen's death (read Acts 7:51).

The so-called "unpardonable sin" was committed only by the Jews who attributed the miracles of Jesus to the power of Satan instead of to the Holy Spirit. This was blasphemy against the Holy Spirit, as spoken of in Luke 12:10. The only "unpardonable sin" that can be committed today, in this dispensation, is that of continued and final rejection of the Lord Jesus Christ, and the refusal to accept Him as Saviour until it is too late. The expression, "unpardonable sin" nowhere occurs in the Bible.

341. Why Is the Blame of Sin Placed on Adam When Eve Partook First of the Forbidden Fruit?

Your question in regard to Adam and Eve can be answered, I believe, by referring to I Timothy 2:14 where we are told that Adam was "not deceived," but the woman "was deceived." The reason the blame of sin is laid upon Adam is that he heard the prohibition concerning the tree before Eve had been created (Genesis 2:17). Eve did not hear God forbid the eating of the tree, but undoubtedly received her information from Adam. Moreover, Eve sinned as a mere individual, while Adam sinned as the head and representative of the entire human race.

342. What Is "A-Millennialism?"

In regard to the theory of A-millennialism, I do not believe that there is anyone who really understands it. It is a subterfuge and escape for post-millennialists and modernists. When two wars in one generation upset the empty dream of post-millennialists, they took refuge in and revived the theory of A-millennialism. No one who knows the Bible believes in the A-millennialism theory. A-millennialism is incipient modernism.

343. Please Explain to Me the Expression, "Salvation and Works."

While our salvation is complete when we receive the Lord Jesus Christ by faith through His finished work, there is much to do after we are saved. This is where much of our preaching has failed in the past. We have been too inclined to forget that because our salvation is done for us, we are to do more for Him. We are told to "work

out our salvation." We believe to be the Lord's desire
that we should work out that which He has already worked
in.

344. How Do You Reconcile Predestination and the Free Will of Man?

While we do not believe that God predestinates anyone
to be lost, in that we are all free moral agents to choose
or reject, nevertheless, we cannot escape the fact that God
does foreknow all things. You are, of course, dealing with
a difficult subject which I believe we will only fully
understand when we reach glory. We are not required
to *reconcile* predestination and free will. We are expected
to *believe* it.

345. What Is Your Stand Concerning "A-Millennialism"?

Concerning the A-millennialist view, I reject vigorously
this view because it is absolutely contrary to the Scriptures.
The A-millennialist believes as the name implies, that there
will be no millennium whatsoever. He completely ignores
the six times the Holy Spirit mentions "a thousand years"
in the twentieth chapter of Revelation. He also ignores the
fact that throughout all the Old Testament prophecies,
God promises the re-establishment of the Messianic Kingdom and the age of peace and prosperity. An A-millennialist who believes in no millennium at all, is simply an individual who used to be a post-millennialist, but because
of the recent developments in the world, this view cannot
be consistently held, and because they will not accept the
Scriptural, pre-millennial view, they slip into A-millennialism. Personally, I believe that A-millennialism is the first
step toward modernism. A-millennialists do not believe
that the Jews are going to be gathered back into Palestine,
or that the Lord Jesus Christ is going to set up His literal,
millennial Kingdom here on earth. Since they do not be-

lieve this, I cannot endorse their view at all. The recent return of the Jews to Palestine absolutely destroys the unscriptural, man-made theory of A-millennialism.

346. What is the Difference Between the Sabbath and the Lord's Day?

Saturday is still the Jewish sabbath, but certainly not the Christian's. Sunday is *not* a sabbath, but the Lord's Day and the day of resurrection. Saturday Christ spent in death; on the first day He rose from death. Christians are not under the curse of the death of the law, but are under the life of Christ. The sabbath was a command to Israel. The Lord's day is a privilege for Christians. The sabbath has never been changed.

347. What Is the Difference Between "Election" and "Predestination?"

Election deals primarily with our salvation, while predestination deals with God's purpose for those who are already elected. God elects His chosen ones to be saved (I Peter 1:2) and then predestinates these elected ones to become like Jesus (Romans 8:29) Both were conceived in the eternity of God's foreknowledge.

348. Can There Be True Faith Without Repentance?

Repentance and faith are inseparable. Repentance without faith is useless, and faith without repentance is impossible. They are "twins," inseparable twins.

349. Will the Heathen Go to Hell?

If you will read carefully Paul's epistle to the Romans, 1:19, 20, you will see that Paul proves there that the heathen are without excuse, because while they have not had the Gospel or the law or the revelations of Scripture and the privileges of civilization, they are guilty because

they have not even followed the light of nature which they
did have. Even without the law or the Gospel, they had the
book of nature. "The heavens declare the glory of God,
and the firmament showeth forth His handiwork." They
are guilty because they have failed to live up to their own
light. God will judge every man according to the opportunity he has had. The more light rejected, the greater
the judgment; the less light rejected, the milder the
punishment, but God is so holy that He must judge all
ungodliness and unrighteousness of men.

God will deal with the heathen in righteousness. If
they have rejected the light they had, they will be
judged and they will be lost, but the degree of their punishment will be according to righteousness and justice.
While we believe that all men are lost without Christ, we
believe that the degree of eternal suffering will be on the
basis of light rejected. In Revelation 20, the dead at the
judgment of the Great White Throne are judged according
to their works. That determines the degree of their punishment — their works. But the fact of their punishment is
determined by their rejection of the light of God, be that
great or be that little. There will be as many degrees of
punishment in hell; as there will be degrees of rewards
in heaven.

350. Please Explain to Me the Difference Between "The Kingdom of God," "The Kingdom of Heaven," and "The Mystery of the Kingdom."

"The Kingdom of God" is the eternal rule of God over
the earth and the nations through all the ages.

"The Kingdom of Heaven" is the dispensation of the
Millennial Kingdom under the rule of Christ when He
personally reigns upon the earth for one thousand years,
and this is part of the Kingdom of God.

"The Mystery of the Kingdom" is the dispensation between Calvary and the Coming of Christ, during which the Kingdom itself is postponed, and the Church takes her place as the mystery during the postponement. This is a mystery to the Old Testament saint and the New Testament sinner.

351. What Is a Parable?

A parable is a method of teaching employed by Jesus, designed to hide the truth from those that should not believe, while revealing the truth to those who would believe. Read Matthew 13:13, Mark 4:11-12 and John 12:37-40.

352. When Does the Soul Enter the Body?

There are several theories which theologians have put forth as to the origin of the soul, and the time it enters the body of the infant. In general, there are three, as follows:

First, there is the Eternal Creationist Theory, which states that in the beginning God created all the souls of all men, and the child receives its soul when it is born.

Second, there is the Developmental Theory, meaning that the soul develops like the body, and is transmitted to the body sometime during the period of gestation, usually considered sometime after the fifth month.

And thirdly, there is the Individual Creationist Theory, which states that God creates one by one a special soul for each body, and that the soul enters the body at conception. Should the child not be born, God gives it a body at the resurrection.

These are matters which only eternity will clear up and reveal to us. The best we can do is to leave it in the hands of an all-wise God.

353. What Is Revival?

Revival has primarily to do with those who are already believers. A sinner cannot be revived. He needs a resurrection, since he is "dead in trespasses and sins." Therefore, when we speak of revival, we must of necessity have people who are already alive spiritually and can be revived. Strictly speaking, revival is an awakening of believers resulting in a cleansing of lives, and a renewed dedication and full surrender to the service of the Lord. When this happens, sinners will be saved.

354. Is the Holy Spirit a Person?

We believe that the Holy Spirit is a Person, for two main reasons, although there are others.

The first reason is that He is addressed as a Person. In our King James version sometimes "He" is referred to as "it," but in every case it should be translated *"He,"* since the masculine is used in the original, and not the neuter. Since He is spoken of as a Person, and referred to in the personal pronoun, we accept this as the first proof.

Then too, the attributes of personality are attributed to the work of the Holy Spirit. For instance, we are told not to "grieve" the Holy Spirit, nor to "resist" the Holy Spirit, etc. Now, of course, we cannot do these things unless He is a Person. We cannot sin against an influence. It has to be a Person.

Upon these and other arguments we base our belief, that the Holy Spirit is a Person exactly as the Father and Jesus Christ the Son. I realize that these theological matters are not always easy to understand, but we have to receive a great many things in the Word of God by faith, and faith begins where reason ends. I am sure that if we continue to search the Scriptures, that we will be made to know the truth. This is His promise.

355. What Is the Meaning of "Sanctification" in the Scriptures?

The word, "sanctification," is used in three different ways in Scripture. First, it means to "set aside for a definite service." A person, objects and articles may be set aside for this purpose. Secondly, sanctification is an immediate act of God whereby we as believers are perfect, *positionally*, in Christ. Then, thirdly, there is the practical sanctification, which is the daily "growing in grace" of God's children who have by faith accepted His finished work.

356. I Am Confused Over the Terms in Scripture, Namely: "The Day of the Lord," "The Day of Christ," and "The Day of God." Do these All Refer to the Same Time, or Is There a Different Meaning for Each?

The phrase, "the day of the Lord," always refers in Scripture to the tribulation period, and is the time of judgment for the Jews on earth. "The day of Christ" has reference to the return of Christ and His millennial reign on earth with the Church. "The day of God" is the end of the world, and the time of judgment of the wicked Gentiles.

357. How Were the Gentiles Saved in the Old Testament, Before Calvary?

Concerning the Gentiles in the Old Testament, there were many Gentiles who were saved in the Old Testament and are called "proselytes" in the Scriptures. While the Gentile nations were not recognized, individual Gentiles could be saved. They were then circumcized and received as proselytes into the assembly of Israel.

358. How Can We Reconcile "Sinless Perfection" with I John 1:10?

In regard to your question, there must be a distinction between the two natures. The *new* nature which we receive when we accept Christ *cannot sin,* but the *old* nature (what we are by our first birth) is with us until we die, and that *always sins.* In I John 1:8-10, John is speaking of the old nature, born of Adam. In I John 3:10, John is speaking of the new nature, born of God.

359. Will the Unsaved All Receive the Same Punishment, or Will There Be Degrees of Punishment?

Concerning the unsaved receiving the same punishment, the Bible plainly teaches that there will be degrees of punishment, depending upon the light which men and women have had, and rejected while here upon the earth (see Luke 12:47-48 and also Revelation 20:12-13).

360. What Is Meant by the Word, "Church"?

The word, "church," is used in two different senses in the Bible. First of all, there is the church universal, consisting of all believers since the day of Pentecost, no matter what their color or condition or nationality or denominational affiliation may be. They are members of the body of Christ which is His Church.

Then, the word, "church," is also used to designate a local company of believers who may be meeting for fellowship. So we read in the Bible about the churches in Corinth, Galatia and Rome. These were local assemblies and were only a part of the true Church as far as the redeemed are concerned. It is well to remember that all members of the church universal are saved. All members of the local church are not necessarily saved. We know that there are also "tares among the wheat."

361. I Have a Real Problem Trying to Teach My Children About God and Who He Is. They Seem to Form a False Conception of What I Am Actually Trying to Teach Them. Can You Help Me?

There are many false and erroneous conceptions of God, and it is not easy to present to small children just exactly what God is in Spirit and in Truth because of the

immaturity of their minds. However, you must remember
that God speaks in the Scripture in anthropo-morphic
terms. God is presented in the Scripture as having hands,
feet, eyes and ears. We realize that these terms are not
to be literally accepted, but God, realizing that we are
human beings, and that we cannot form a mental concept of
things without material form, has condescended to present
His Power under the figure of the eyes of the Lord, the
ears of the Lord, the hands of the Lord, etc. We are not to
visualize God as a "Big Man," but these terms and ex-
pressions through their physical figure present to us a
picture of the power and the ability of Almighty God. Of
course, we cannot present this to small children, but as
they grow older we can tell them that these things are a
spiritual picture of what God is able to do in our lives.

362. What Are "Church Creeds," and Where Did the Church Get "the Apostle's Creed?"

Creeds are simply statements which various churches
or denominations have adopted as a sort of a form which
they follow. They are not inspired like the Bible, and do
not speak with any authority, such as the Scriptures do.
Every church seems to have its own creed.

The Apostle's Creed is one of the older ones, but you
must not be misled by the name, "Apostle's Creed," for the
apostles themselves had absolutely nothing to do with the
formulation of this statement. It was drawn up by church
men many, many years after all of the apostles were dead,
so it is just a matter of each denomination choosing its
own creed. There are various versions of it. The two best-
known creeds, of course, are the ones called "The Apostles'
Creed," and "The Athanasian Creed," so-called because a
certain theologian by the name of Athanasius drew it up.

363. What Is Meant by "Urim and Thummim" Found in Exodus 28:30?

It is not certain what the Urim and the Thummim are in the Bible. Theologians have speculated on it again and again, but no one seems to know definitely. It is, therefore, one of those matters about which we will have to wait until we get to glory.

364. What Is the Difference Between Jews and Hebrews?

Abraham before he was called in Genesis 12, was a Syrian who according to the Bible came from an idolatrous family. Then when he came into Canaan, he became the first Hebrew. The word, "Hebrew," means to "cross over," and it comes from the fact that Abraham crossed over from Syria into Palestine. All the descendants from Abraham, therefore, can properly be called Hebrews. However, the word, "Jew," refers especially to the remnant of the southern kingdom of Judah who returned after the captivity in Babylon. The descendants of all the twelve tribes are Hebrews, while the descendants of the southern kingdom are particularly the Jewish people.

365. What Is the Difference between the Soul and the Spirit?

The soul is the part of man which resulted from the union of spirit and body. Our body links us to the material creation. Our soul links us to God's intelligent creation, and therefore, is the seat of fellowship and praise. The spirit links us with God. When Christ died, His body went to the tomb; He committed His spirit into the hands of God, and His soul went into Sheol (see Psalm 16, and Acts 2).

366. How Can the Soul Be Immortal If the Body Dies?

The Bible plainly teaches that the body is mortal, but the soul is immortal. The body dies, and Scripture calls it "asleep," while the soul is never said to sleep. In I Corinthians 15:51-54 the distinction between the living body which is mortal, and the dead body which is corruptible, is clearly made. The Bible everywhere teaches consciousness of the soul after death. Lazarus and the rich man in Luke 16 were certainly conscious.

367. Are the Mind and the Spirit the Same?

The mind has to do more with the soul, while the spirit is that which is the divine nature, according to Peter.

368. Does Man Belong to the Animal Kingdom?

Science divides all matter into mineral, vegetable and animal, and includes man, as far as his physical being is concerned, in the animal kingdom. Science says, therefore, that man is neither vegetable nor mineral, but that he belongs to the animal realm.

However, we must remember, according to Scripture, man is created in the image of God, and as such is set apart from all the rest of the animal kingdom.

CHAPTER 13

HEAVEN

369. Will We Recognize Our Loved Ones in Heaven?

Moses and Elijah were recognized immediately by the disciples in Matthew 17. The rich man in hell recognized Lazarus in the bosom of Abraham. The disciples recognized the Lord Jesus after His resurrection, and in I Thessalonians chapter 4, we are told that we shall be caught up "together with them" (our loved ones) so that there will be perfect recognition in heaven.

370. If All Who Died Before Calvary Went into the Heart of the Earth, How Could Elijah Have Been Caught up into Heaven?

Elijah was caught up into heaven, but it does not say which heaven. There is a difference between heaven and the immediate presence of God. There was in the Old Testament tabernacle a Holy Place and a Holy of Holies. Into the Holy Place all the priests went, but into the Holy of Holies only the High Priest went once a year. We assume that while Elijah was caught into heaven, he was not caught into the immediate presence of God until after Calvary.

371. How Can I Be Happy in Heaven If My Children Are Lost?

Concerning your unsaved children, you must remember that if you will trust the Lord, you have His promise, "believe on the Lord Jesus Christ, and thou shalt be saved, *and thy house*" (Acts 16:31). You must not go on the

assumption that they are *not* going to be saved. You must
by faith accept the promise that they *will* be saved. Then
your question concerning being in heaven while your children are lost need never come up. When we get to heaven,
we shall understand that everything God does is just, no
matter what it may be.

372. What Will Be Our Family Relationship in Heaven?

We will undoubtedly know our fathers and mothers
and children, but our relationship with Christ will be so
much higher and far above our earthly relationships, that
all of these others will be subject to and explained by our
relationship to Him.

373. What Kind of Body Will the Resurrected Saint Have?

We believe that the bodies of the resurrected saints will
be like unto the body of the Lord Jesus Christ, according to
the book of Philippians (Phil. 3:21). Since the body of the
Lord Jesus Christ was a mature body at about the age of 33
when He arose, we have reason to believe that our bodies
will be like that. We shall be able to eat, but not of necessity. These new bodies will not be subject to natural
laws, but spiritual.

374. Can Our Loved Ones in Heaven See Us Here?

In regard to your question concerning the knowledge of
our loved ones who have died in the faith about things happening here upon earth, it is quite evident from the first
verse of the twelfth chapter of Hebrews that they do have
knowledge of things which are happening here below. We
are told there that we are surrounded by "so great a cloud
of witnesses," and the very fact that they are witnessing
what we are doing is our incentive to work and run the
race faithfully before God. The Lord Jesus also said that
there was joy in the presence of the angels of God over

one sinner that repenteth (Luke 15:7). However, this truth should not disturb us in the least, for the simple reason that they will see things through the eyes of eternity and through the eyes of the Lord, and will understand all things in the light of the providence and the righteousness and the wisdom of God. So they do not look at things as we look at them here, but knowing much more than we do, are able to understand and submit themselves in all dealings to the Lord.

375. Is Heaven an Actual Place?

I am sorry that you have been somewhat confused in regard to the matter of heaven. Heaven is *not* a state or condition, but heaven is definitely *a place*. Remember that the Lord Jesus Christ ascended into heaven with a resurrection body. This body was a body that could be seen and touched, a real body. Therefore, heaven must be a place.

376. Will There Be Children in Heaven?

Concerning children in heaven, there is not much in the Bible concerning conditions in heaven, and we do not know exactly just what all of us will be like when we get there. However, there is a great deal in the Bible telling us about the conditions during the millennium, the one thousand years of peace, when Christ shall reign here upon the earth.

According to Isaiah and Zechariah, children will continue to be born during this millennial period, and we read in Zechariah that the streets of Jerusalem shall be full of boys and girls playing upon the streets thereof. However, we must remember that the millennium is on the earth, and not in heaven. Evidently the Lord does not want us to know just what conditions in heaven will be, so that we may have a real surprise when we get there.

It is comforting to know, however, that all children who die before the age of responsibility do go to heaven, and none of them are lost. We must be careful not to speculate beyond that which has been revealed in the Word of God. We do know that during the millennium, many, many children will be born into the world. As to their status in heaven, we do not know, but we shall know some day.

377. I Am Wondering If the Expression, "Stars in Our Crown," Is Scriptural.

In regard to your question concerning "stars in our crown," I do not find anything in the entire Bible to warrant anything of the kind. It is just a fantasy of some poetic mind who thought it up, and there certainly is nothing in the Bible to indicate that such things will happen. I do not believe that it is important, but if we are to be strictly Scriptural, there is no ground for it.

378. If We Are Caught Up to Be with the Lord Before the Tribulation Period, How Can We Be Happy There While We View the Terrible Destruction on Earth to Those Who Are Left Behind?

We must remember that when we get to heaven, we will look at things through the eyes of God. We will not view things in the light of our fleshly nature here below, but we will see everything in the light of God's righteousness and justice and truth. How can God be happy in heaven when so many of His creatures, for whom Christ died, will not come to Him? He views it in the light of His righteousness, and we will look at things in that same light.

379. Do All Babies Go to Heaven?

The Bible does not have too much to say concerning the condition of babies in heaven. However, we do believe that all children who die before the age of accountability are saved, since they have never had the opportunity of re-

jecting the Gospel of the Lord Jesus Christ or the light that
God has given to them. We believe that Jesus died on the
Cross of Calvary for the sins of mankind, and today only
one sin can condemn a man, and that is the sin of wilfully
rejecting the message which God gives to fallen man. I believe with all my heart that every baby that dies, whether
before birth or after birth, before it reaches the age of
accountability, goes to heaven, and we shall meet them
again. Just at what time the soul enters the body the Bible
does not state, and we must leave this entirely with the
Lord.

380. Will We Eat in Heaven?

To this question we can answer both no and yes. The
souls of the saints now in heaven probably do not eat at this
time, for they have no physical bodies, but we are sure that
when Jesus comes again and all the saints receive their
new resurrection bodies that we shall indeed eat. We
shall not need to eat, for there we shall hunger no more,
neither thirst any more; but we can and we will eat. Jesus
proved His humanity, you will remember, after His resurrection, by eating before His disciples on the shores of the
sea of Galilee in His resurrection body. Yes, there is food
in heaven, manna, and at least twelve different kinds of
fruits on the one tree of life which grew on either side
of the river of life. Eating will be one of the joys of
heaven.

381. Are Enoch, Moses and Elijah the Only Old Testament Saints Now in Heaven?

Concerning Enoch, Moses and Elijah, they are not the
only ones in heaven now, since the resurrection of Jesus
Christ. Matthew 27:52-53 tells us of another group who
were raised at the resurrection of our Lord, and presuma-
bly went to heaven with Jesus as the "firstfruits of the
resurrection."

CHAPTER 14

MARRIAGE, DIVORCE AND RE-MARRIAGE

382. According to Deuteronomy 24:1-2, It Seems That God Permitted Divorce. Can You Help Me to Understand This Passage in the Light of the New Testament Teaching on Divorce?

This entire matter is cleared up when we read in Matthew 19:4 where our Lord says "He which made them in the beginning, made them male and female," and in the eighth verse, "Moses, because of the hardness of your hearts, suffered you to put away your wives; but from the beginning it was not so," and then adds, "Whosoever shall put away his wife, excepting it be for fornication, and shall marry another, committeth adultery." Certainly these words are clear that while Moses suffered it because of the wickedness of Israel, it was never right, and today Jesus is clear in stating in His Word that divorce is always wrong, and can only be obtained on one ground, and then the parties are never to remarry as long as both are alive.

383. From Both the Medical and Scriptural Standpoint, What Do You Believe Concerning the Inter-Marriage of Close Relatives?

It is generally understood that the marriage of close blood relations is often followed by degenerate offspring, and the best authorities advise strongly against it.

The Bible specifically prohibits the marriage of those who are near relatives. In this connection, I think you will find what the Bible has to say in Leviticus 18:6, Leviticus 20:19 and Leviticus 25:49 helpful. Moreover, besides the

Biblical prohibition, it is also the opinion of medical men and physiologists that marriage of relatives as near as cousins is to be discouraged for reasons of its effect upon the offspring. From this it would seem that cousins ought never to marry.

384. According to I Corinthians 7:32 It Seems That Paul Considered Those Who Remained Unmarried More Spiritual. What Did He Mean by This?

In regard to I Corinthians 7:32, we must remember that Paul was writing at a time when persecution was great and the Christians were being oppressed to a point where it seemed that they could not go on. In the light of all this, Paul said what he did about marriage. However, Paul also said that marriage is honorable in all, and even urged in Timothy that the younger women marry and bear children. You must always take these Scriptures in the light of the circumstances in which they are written.

385. I Married a Divorced Man When I Was in a Backslidden Condition. I Have Now Come Back to the Lord, and Am Wondering in Order to Make Restitution for My Sin If I Should Leave My Husband, Since His First Wife Is Still Living.

Since you have made the mistake after you were a Christian, we believe the Lord does forgive, but we have to be willing to pay the price which is sometimes mighty dear. You will, undoubtedly, have to carry the reproach of conscience throughout your life as the penalty for your mistake. It is difficult for us to tell you just what to do. I suggest that you continue to pray about it, and be careful that you do not add another mistake to the one already made. May God give you wisdom and understanding in this difficult problem, and may the Spirit of the Lord direct you, and His blessing rest upon you.

386. I Was Divorced and Re-married Before I Became a Christian. Recently in Studying the Word I Have Become convinced of the Sin of Divorce and Re-marriage and Am Concerned About This Matter and Its Effect Upon My Testimony.

I have always held the position that if the sin of divorce and remarriage is committed before people are saved, the Lord puts it under the blood just like any other sin. I, therefore, believe that you should forget about it, and try to do your best in serving the Lord.

387. I Am a Divorced Person, Re-married. I Have Been Teaching a Sunday School Class in My Church, but Recently Have Been Questioning My Right to This Position in the Church. I Want to Be in the Lord's Will.

I cannot pass judgment on your individual case, but I feel that divorce should never occur among Christians. However, when it does occur, they must be willing to pay the penalty. In your case, there seems to be a difference since you were still unsaved at the time of the divorce and re-marriage. I am sure that you realize that divorce is not the will of the Lord, but if He opens the door for your service, I do not see any reason why you should not do what you can in this work of the Lord, as long as it is not a reproach upon the testimony of Christ.

388. What Do You Think of Marriage between Protestants and Catholics?

I do not believe that we should ever encourage marriage between Protestants and Catholics. We have no right to believe that any Catholic or Protestant is a Christian until they have been truly born again. Just believing with the head certain truths of the Bible, or going to church, does not make one a Christian. One must have a definite, personal experience of salvation and have accepted Christ as his own personal Saviour. I do not feel that you can expect the Lord's blessing upon any union between a Protestant Christian and one who is a Catholic. Experience over many years has taught that they usually end in disaster and are most unhappy.

CHAPTER 15

MEDICAL QUESTIONS

389. Do You Believe in Divine Healing?

We do believe that Christ can and does heal when it is His will to do so. However, there is much of unscriptural profiteering and racketeering under the name of healing, against which we should guard. This is not the age of healing, but the age of grace and faith. "For the Jews require a sign, and the Greeks seek after wisdom: But we preach Christ crucified" (I Cor. 1:22-23). Anyone who claims the gift of healing today is a fraud and a deceiver. The apostolic gifts are not for this age.

390. Does Isaiah 53:4 Teach Divine Healing of the Body? I Heard a Preacher Say That the Correct Translation of Isaiah 53:4 Should be "He Hath Borne Our Sicknesses and Carried Our Diseases." Does This Refer To Physical Sickness?

Yes, that is quite correct. The reference is to the literal bodily sickness, but this verse was not fulfilled on the Cross of Calvary, and is, therefore, no argument for divine healing today, in the atonement. The 8th chapter of Matthew tells us very clearly that this prophecy was fulfilled before Calvary during the life and the ministry of the Lord Jesus Christ. When Jesus went about healing the sick, Matthew tells us that he "healed all that were sick: That it *might be fulfilled* which was spoken by Esaias the prophet, saying, Himself took our infirmities, and bare our sicknesses." (Matt. 8:16-17) From this you will see that this prophecy was fulfilled while Jesus was ministering here upon the earth, healing the sick.

191

391. Should We Call a Physician When Someone Is Ill?

We believe that the Lord is able to heal today as well as at any other time, but it must be according to His will. Jesus said when He was here on earth, in Matthew 9:12, "They that be whole need not a physician, but they that are sick." Therefore, we should call a physician in case of illness. When you cut your finger you wrap a bandage around it; that is using the means. You do not expect the Lord to stop the bleeding and heal the finger when it is cut, without treating it. We should apply this principle to all other diseases. We believe that God can and does heal, but we also are expected to use the means which He has given.

392. Our Little Boy Has Been Stricken with Infantile Paralysis, and We Are Much Concerned. Since You Are a Doctor As Well As a Preacher, We Should Appreciate Any Words of Help or Encouragement You Can Give Us.

In regard to your boy, it is essential that you follow the proper advice and treatment for infantile paralysis. Infantile paralysis is a disease caused by a virus which is infectious and usually gains entrance through the mucous membrane of the nose and throat. The disease itself affects the part of the spinal column which contains the motor nerves and so when the victim is attacked it often causes paralysis. It is impossible to recommend any remedy unless one knows exactly what the extent of the disease is. Good food and fresh air are essential, although the diet is not the important thing.

The best advice I can give you is to trust the Lord and then keep under the care of a good physician, probably a specialist, who will advise as to diet, medications, massage and general treatment. It is impossible to give important advice without a thorough examination of the case.

393. I Am Afflicted with Diabetes, and My Doctor Has Advised Me Not to Have Any More Children. What Does the Bible Have to Say Concerning Birth Control?

In regard to your problem concerning birth control, I do not believe that the Bible sanctions it. However, in your condition, being a diabetic, I think the Lord would have you follow the advice of your doctor and not jeopardize your position as a wife and a mother by having any more children.

394. Was Bodily Healing in the Atonement?

I do not believe that healing was in the atonement in the same sense that sin was taken care of, although I do believe the Lord is able to heal if it is His will. We can pray God for healing and then use the means which He has given.

In a certain sense bodily healing is in the atonement. So is the ultimate resurrection and redemption of my body, but it will not occur until Jesus comes again to shout from the air at His second coming. In Isaiah 53:5, the prophet is not talking about bodily healing of disease, but about the healing of the disease of sin. This is again made crystal-clear by the Apostle Peter who quotes this very verse, so there can be no question as to its meaning. God's Word is always its own best interpreter. In this connection, read I Peter 2:24.

> Who his own self bare our sins in his own body on the tree, that we, being dead to sins, should live unto righteousness: by whose stripes ye were healed (I Peter 2:24).

Peter is talking about sins, and is speaking about the healing of these sins. There is no thought at all here of bodily healing. It is *sin* he is dealing with. However, I do not want to be misunderstood. There is not a doubt in my mind that God is able to heal without any means at all if it is His will. No sincere Christian doubts this fact. But to say that God must heal is to dictate to Him and is wicked and wholly contrary to the Bible.

395. Are Christians Supposed to Have As Many Children As Possible?

Your question seems to be just a little indefinite. I do believe that when circumstances warrant and health permits, that the Lord expects us to follow His command, "Multiply and be fruitful." Where these conditions do not exist, we are to follow the Scriptural method of control, remembering that the only Scriptural birth control is self-control.

396. Do You Think That Drugs and Medicines Should Be Used by Christians?

In regard to your question concerning drugs, I see no reason why we should not use the elements which God has placed in nature for our benefit. This, of course, always must be with moderation, and only when indicated specifically. Both in the Old and New Testament the use of medicines is sanctioned and recommended.

397. I Am a Christian and My Wife Is Not. We Are Expecting Our First Child, and My Wife Is a Heavy Smoker. Will This Affect Our Child?

In regard to your wife's condition, there is a difference of opinion about smoking affecting the unborn child, either in carrying it or in the feeding of the baby. Your only solution seems to be to continue to trust the Lord, not to doubt Him, and to claim His promise concerning her. Your greatest concern should be her salvation, and then all these other matters will be solved.

398. What Is Your Opinion Concerning Psycho-Analysis and Psychotherapy in the Life of a Christian?

In regard to psycho-analysis and psycho-therapy in the life of a Christian, these have the same place in treating disease that other medical and surgical methods have. It is generally believed that many ailments of people today are mental and have to do with the mind. As such, the doctor looks at these patients as being mentally sick rather than physically sick, and instead of ministering the ordinary physical remedies, they try to apply mental and psychic treatments.

As is often the case, the thing has been entirely over-rated and it has gone to an absurd extreme, so that there is sometimes great difficulty in knowing whether it is of any value whatsoever. These new things always tend to swing to a tremendous extreme and after a while seem to come back to normal. The sad part of it all is that these things have to be administered by men who do not believe in God, and do not believe in the Lord Jesus Christ. I do believe, however, that if a Christian physician who is thoroughly schooled in this branch of medical science administers it, there can be no harm done.

399. Is Tuberculosis Mentioned in the Bible?

Tuberculosis is not mentioned by name in the Bible anywhere. As the germ which causes leprosy is a bacillus which closely resembles the tuberculosis germ, it is be-believed by some that there may be some relationship between the two. Beyond this, we have no intimation to believe that tuberculosis is mentioned in Scripture.

400. What Is Your Opinion Concerning Drinking Tea and Coffee?

The matter of drinking tea or coffee is entirely a question of personal conscience. If a person thinks it is wrong, then it is wrong. If they have no conscience in the matter, no one is allowed to judge. I Corinthians 8 will answer your question, I am sure. Naturally this refers to the moderate use, and not the abuse. Also read carefully Romans 14:13.

401. Since You Are a Physician As Well As a Minister, I Would Like Your Views Concerning the Use of Whiskey As a Medicine.

For medicinal purposes and in medicinal doses only, there can be no harm in using a little whiskey. In fact, most of the liquid preparations, including cough syrups, contain alcohol, needed for preserving as well as a solvent for other drugs. Alcohol medicinally is used quite extensively in doses which are beneficial, rather than deleterious.

402. I Have a Disabled Hand, and the Doctor Tells Me I Should Undergo Surgery. I Am Wondering If I Should Follow His Advice, or Just Trust the Lord to Heal Me.

In regard to your disabled hand, you realize that it is quite difficult to give definite advice unless one knows all the circumstances and also the report of the X-ray. However, we must realize that while the Lord is able to heal, He also uses the means through physicians and surgeons. They too are the gift of God. Jesus said, "They that are whole have no need of a physician but they that are sick." I would, therefore, if I were you, abide by the report of the doctor who has the X-ray findings, and if it is necessary to operate, I would not object at all.

While we believe the Lord is able to heal without means, this may not be His will. The Lord could also keep us without eating, but it is His plan that we should eat to sustain our life. We shall be praying for you that the Lord may lead you, and that you may find complete relief. However, I do not believe that it is displeasing to the Lord to go to a surgeon if he can help you.

403. I Have Been Reading and Hearing a Lot Concerning the Dr. Koch Treatment for Cancer, and Since You Are a Doctor, Wondered What Information You Could Give Me Concerning This.

For details concerning Dr. Koch, see the April, 1950, issue of *Readers Digest,* article entitled "Beware the Scientific Medical Quacks!" beginning at page 68 especially, which exposes this movement denounced by the American Medical Association. This article will give you authentic data concerning this treatment.

404. Someone Told Me That Nine Out of Ten People Who Are Insane Are Demon Possessed. I Would Like to Have Your Opinion Concerning This Statement, Since You Are a Physician As Well As a Minister.

There is absolutely no truth whatsoever in the statement that nine out of ten people who are insane are demon possessed. During the days of Jesus there was unusual activity among the demons. However, today we believe that it is exceedingly rare. I do not deny that it is possible, but I personally have never seen a case of actual demon possession. Every case of insanity could be diagnosed on the basis of mental or physical grounds.

405. If We Put Ourselves Under the Care of a Doctor, How Can We Also Have Our Trust in the Lord, Since We Are Looking to Man for Our Healing.

In regard to your question concerning trusting a doctor and the Lord at the same time, you must remember that while all healing is of the Lord, He has also given us means and given wisdom to men to use this means placed at our disposal. The Lord Jesus Christ said emphatically that when we are sick we should call a doctor (See Matthew 9:12). Of course, in all of this we acknowledge the fact that the Lord is the one who gives the wisdom and the only One who can bless the means. We know that God can heal without means, but also that He usually uses the means.

406. Does the Lord Perform Miracles Today Such As When He Was Here?

To answer this, we must remember that there are no miracles with God. They are miracles only with men. A miracle occurs when God suspends the natural way of doing things, and acts in the supernatural, instead of in the natural way. In John 2, Jesus turned water into wine. Now turning water into wine in itself is no miracle. It happens all the time as the vine takes up the water from the ground, and by the aid of the sunshine and life and elements in its solution, this water in the grape becomes wine in the end. This naturally takes about five months. But Jesus, the Creator, accelerated this process so that instead of taking five months, it happened instantly. That is no more mysterious than the growth of grapes on a vine, but because it is the unusual, we call it a miracle.

407. Do You Recommend Innoculations for Children?

As a physician I can say that innoculations for diphtheria, whooping cough and small pox are extremely successful, and there is no danger associated with them at all. It was these diseases which, when I was first practicing medicine many years ago, took such a toll of lives but today are almost entirely unheard of. I certainly recommend it very highly.

In regard to tetanus, the effect wears off rather soon, but it is valuable. I do not believe that innoculation for tetanus is so important in infants as in the matter of diphtheria, whooping cough and small pox.

408. What Is the Reason for Not Performing Circumcision before the Eighth Day As Commanded in God's Word?

In regard to the matter of circumcision, it has been definitely shown that if children are circumcised before the eighth day, there is danger of hemorrhage developing because the blood-clotting elements of the blood have not yet been manufactured. If the circumcision is done at any length of time after the eighth day, there is danger of infection, since the anti-bodies which are received from the mother at birth gradually diminish, and the child does not have the resistance to disease after that, that it would have before. That is why the Lord commanded it to be done on the eighth day. Of course, this does not mean that anyone who is circumcised before the eighth day will necessarily have a hemorrhage, or one who is circumcised after the eighth day will develop infection, but merely that the danger and the possibility is greater.

409. Here Is Something That Worries Me. Doctors Give People Medicine That Makes Them Dizzy and Puts Them to Sleep So They Do Not Know What Is Going On, and I Have Also Heard That Strong Drinks Will Knock a Person Out. Would There Be Any Difference in the Two? Would It Be Wrong to Take Medicine That Makes a Person Feel Dizzy but Stops Pain in Childbirth, or Should We Just Suffer?

Concerning your problem, you must remember that way back in the beginning, in Genesis 2:21 we have a record of the very first operation in history, and there God caused a deep sleep to fall upon Adam, and while he slept, God removed one of his ribs, and then closed up the flesh. Of course, the Bible does not say what God used to cause this sleep, but whatever it was, it served the same purpose that the medical men use today to perform operations, etc. I trust that these few words will be of help to you in this matter about which you have been worrying.

410. If We Try to Follow the Practices Mentioned in Leviticus 15 Concerning Birth Control, Would We Not Be Going Back to the Law?

In regard to your question concerning birth control, I feel that the only birth control which the Bible teaches is that which is found in the book of Leviticus. This, of course, does not mean birth *prevention*, but only birth *control*. If this technique is followed, the Lord Himself will determine the spacing of the children, and also how many children there should be in the family. If this order is not followed, then, of course, the number of children as well as the spacing of the children is determined by the individual, and this is quite unscriptural. I am sure that it is much better to have the Lord decide how many and how far apart these children should come, and I feel that this rule in Leviticus is still binding today.

While we believe that the Law was fulfilled in Christ, we must remember that the principles laid down in the Old Testament are still in effect. Many of the laws of hygiene and sanitation and cleansing as well as dietary laws and laws of government and jurisprudence are still the word of the Living God. I feel that the same thing is true in regard to this matter of birth control. It is entirely a matter of whether we want to take the Word of the Lord, or to set up our own standard in regard to this matter.

There is only one Biblical method of birth prevention, and that is abstinence; and only one Biblical method of birth control, which is self-control. I find no authority in the Word of God for the use of mechanical or chemical preventatives in this matter. I believe it to be contrary to the Word of God, and in violation of His command, "be ye fruitful and multiply, and replenish the earth."

CHAPTER 16

MILLENNIUM

411. I Heard You Say Once On a Broadcast That There Would Be Children Born on Earth During the Millennium. Can You Give Me More Light On This?

Isaiah 11:8 and Zechariah 8:5 both speak of the millennium and will show you what we mean, as well as Isaiah 65:20. These chapters are a description of the millennial kingdom and are clear in teaching there will be multitudes of children born during this age.

412. During the Millennium When the Saints Reign with Christ on the Earth, Will Their Bodies Be Visible?

Your question concerning the visibility of saints during the millennium can be answered in the affirmative by reminding you that the Lord Jesus Christ also will be visible. He was visible in His resurrection body to His disciples when He went up into heaven, and when He comes back again. Even though the resurrection body is a spiritual body, it is nevertheless tangible and visible. Even the Lord could eat in His resurrection body.

413. Who Will Live on the Earth During the Millennium?

During the millennium saved nations shall live on the earth, but children who are born will have to be saved by faith in the Lord Jesus Christ, just as today. Israel will dwell in the land of Canaan, while the saints will reign with Christ over the whole earth.

414. In Regard to the Reign of Christ, Where Will He Reign?

All questions concerning this matter result from the fact that some Bible teachers interpret reigning *on* the

201

earth as meaning *over*. The fact is that Scripture teaches
that the saints shall reign *on* and *over* the earth. Christ
will reign in Jerusalem, and His saints will be with Him
there.

415. What Is Meant by the Phrase in Luke 1:33, "Of His Kingdom There Shall Be No End," If the Millennium Is for One Thousand Years?

The expression, "of his kingdom there shall be no end,"
means simply that while the millennium will last for one
thousand years, the reign will continue on into eternity
after the new heavens and the new earth are created.

416. If the Wicked Are Destroyed at the End of the Tribulation, Who Are the People and Nations That Will Live During the Millennium?

During the millennial age on the cleansed earth, there
will be people in the flesh dwelling on the earth in peace.
During the tribulation all who receive the mark of the
beast will be killed, but there will be nations who refuse the mark of the beast, who will go on into the millennial age. The Lord does spare certain ones, including
the 144,000.

417. Please Give Me Scripture References Concerning the People Who Live During the One Thousand Years.

Concerning the people who live one thousand years, I
would like to refer you to Isaiah 65, verses 20 - 22,
which is a picture of the millennial age. Especially notice
verse 20. Those who at the end of the millennium have
not in their hearts accepted Christ will be cast into the
lake of fire. Those who have believed on Him will go into
eternity as the saved nations of the earth. Revelation 21:24
speaks of these nations also.

418. Will There Be Sickness and Death in the Millennium?

There will be no sickness during the millennium, but there will be death. According to the Scriptures, during the millennium the inhabitants shall not say, "I am sick." Death will be the result of open, wilful rebellion against the reign of Christ. No one will die under one hundred years of age, since life will be prolonged so that infancy will last for one hundred years. Read carefully in this connection Isaiah 55 and 56.

419. Who Will Live in the "New Jerusalem," and Where Will It Be?

The Bible is quite plain that the New Jerusalem will be the abode of the redeemed saints, and it is generally believed that it will be suspended in the air over the earth. During the millennium the saints will reign with Christ upon the earth. During eternity they will continue to reign forever and ever over the earth with headquarters in the New Jerusalem while during the millennium the reign goes forth from the literal Jerusalem in Palestine (see Revelation 20-21).

CHAPTER 17

MISCELLANEOUS QUESTIONS

420. What Is the "Book Of Life"?

The "Book of Life" has given rise to many strange interpretations. Theologians are not all agreed. It is generally taught that all who are born have their names entered in the Book of Life, and when they reject and refuse the Lord Jesus Christ, their name is taken out. Still others teach that a man's name is entered in the Book of Life the moment he believes and accepts Christ as his personal Saviour. It is impossible to say dogmatically just which is right. Since we believe that all babies go to heaven, it would seem logical that their names are recorded in the book of life, but this, of course, depends on the foreknowledge of God.

421. Why Did the Lord Speak in Parables, and What Is the Meaning of the Parable of the Merchantman and the Pearl?

The reason the Lord Jesus Christ spoke in parables will be found in Matthew 13:13-15.

> Therefore speak I to them in parables: because they seeing see not; and hearing they hear not, neither do they understand.
>
> And in them is fulfilled the prophecy of Esaias, which saith, By hearing ye shall hear, and shall not understand; and seeing ye shall see, and shall not perceive:
>
> For this people's heart is waxed gross, and their ears are dull of hearing, and their eyes they have closed; lest at any time they should see with their eyes and hear with their ears, and should understand with their heart, and should be converted, and I should heal them (Matt. 13:13-15).

The parable of the merchantman and the pearl in this thirteenth chapter of Matthew represents the Lord Jesus Christ as the merchantman, and the pearl as the true Church hid in the sea of the nations, but purchased by the Lord Jesus Christ.

422. What Is Meant by the Different Glories Mentioned in the Fifteenth Chapter of I Corinthians?

The different glories, such as that of the sun, moon and stars, refer to the positions of God's people in the millennial age as based upon their works here on earth. This chapter (I Cor. 15) clearly indicates that it refers to our status after the resurrection.

423. Can We Judge the Lives of Other People?

We cannot judge men's hearts, for only God can see that. However, we can judge men's works, for Jesus said, "Wherefore by their fruits ye shall know them" (Matt. 7:20). If a man does not live like a Christian, we have a right to consider him as a sinner, and try to show him the way.

424. In Interpreting the Parable of the Camel and the Needle's Eye, I Heard That the Eye of the Needle Was a Small Gate in the Larger Gate of the City of Jerusalem. Can You Give Me a Clearer Understanding of this Parable Recorded in Matthew 19:24?

> And again I say unto you, It is easier for a camel to go through the eye of a needle, than for a rich man to enter into the kingdom of God (Matt. 19:24).

I am afraid I shall have to disagree in regard to the interpretation of the needle's eye and the camel. I know it is commonly interpreted as meaning a smaller gate in the larger gate of Jerusalem. This means that to get through, the camel would have to get down, take off the load, and wiggle through. In this way it would be possible for a camel to go through the eye of the needle, but the Lord Himself says in this same chapter that this is impossible. What Jesus really said was that it was easier for a literal camel to go through the eye of a literal needle than for a rich man to be saved. With men this is impossible, but with God nothing is impossible, so while riches often turn men away from God, yet in infinite grace many rich have been and are being saved.

425. What Is the Meaning of "Leaven," and What Is the Significance of the Feast of Unleavened Bread?

Leaven in Scripture always means evil and sin, and since the Feast of Unleavened Bread came immediately after the Passover, and just before the Feast of Firstfruits, it evidently refers to the carrying away of our sins by the Lord Jesus Christ. It fits into the picture in no other way than between the Cross and the ressurrection. It teaches separation from sin and sinful practices after we have been saved through the sacrifice of Christ.

426. Is Cremation for the Believer Scriptural, or Is It Forbidden by the Word of God?

Cremation is a pagan practice and there is no sanction given to it in the Bible whatsoever. It is born of the idea that in this way we can prevent God from bringing us back to life again. In every instance in Scripture burial is the proper mode, and the Bible says "Dust thou art, and unto dust thou shalt return," (Genesis 3:19) and the expression in our burial services used by so many preachers who ought to know better, "ashes to ashes," is just a heathen, pagan superstition.

427. Someone Told Me That Planting and Reaping Should Be Done According to the Position of the Moon. Is This Rule Set Forth in the Bible?

Concerning planting and reaping by the moon, I am afraid that I can be of little help to you. Personally, I have always thought it was just a superstition, but I am not enough of a farmer to know. I do not know of anything in Scripture which forbids it, however.

428. What Is the Difference between Apostles and Disciples?

In regard to the difference between an apostle and a disciple, a disciple was one who came after the Lord Jesus as a special envoy. They were representatives of the Lord Jesus Christ. The word "disciple" means a "student" or a "learner." The word "apostle" means "one who goes forth," and literally means in the Greek, "a sent one." The disciples, therefore, were the representatives of the Lord Jesus Christ in a less official and authoritative way. It is possible for us to be disciples of the Lord Jesus Christ, if we are willing to follow Him all the way. It is not possible for us today to be apostles, since they were specially appointed to represent Him in His kingdom message.

429. If Israel Had Accepted the Son of God When He Was on Earth, As Their Messiah, Would the Lord Have Had to Go to the Cross and Shed His Blood for Their Sins?

Your question is one which is frequently asked, but really is not difficult, if you remember that God is omniscient and knew beforehand that Israel would reject her Messiah, and therefore, God could make His plans, taking into account the crucifixion of the Lord Jesus Christ. Of course, since God is all-powerful, if the Jews had accepted the Lord, God would also have had another plan. These things belong to the secret counsel of God, and there are many things that we know, but cannot understand.

430. I Am Upset Concerning My Life and What the Lord Would Have Me Do. How Can I Know His Will for My Life?

In regard to your problem concerning knowing the will of God, it is not one that is always easy to answer. Sometimes the Lord wants to teach us patience and we have to learn to wait upon Him without being able to know definitely what He would have us to do. In a case of that kind, you can only wait upon the Lord, sometimes for a long while, but in the end I am sure that He always makes His way clear. I do not believe that one should be jumping at conclusions and yet when the Lord leads, there is nothing else for us to do. I would suggest that you continue in your present position while continuing to pray for more light, and then when the Lord shows you, I do not believe there will be any doubt in your mind. Remember, we cannot know God's will apart from knowing His Word, so I suggest you study your Bible diligently and continue in prayer. In searching the Scriptures you will find His will for your life.

431. Do You Think That a Saved Person Would Ever Commit Suicide?

I do not believe that those who take their own lives are in their right mind. It is entirely an abnormal thing for people to seek to destroy themselves. Therefore, I believe that they are not responsible, and we have no reason to believe that such folks are not saved. We believe that many of them are. If, before they lost their mind, they had a definite testimony, I do not believe we should worry about them at all. Why God permits His children to do this we cannot understand, any more than we can understand war and many other things which we see round about us.

432. If Paul Was Saved By Grace, Why Did He Observe the Sabbath Day with the Jews? (Acts 18:4)

You must remember that Paul sought to "be all things to all men, if by any means he might win some." Since the Jews congregated in the synagogues on the Sabbath Day, Paul in order to reach them met with them there, but at the same time he also observed the Lord's day with the disciples in the breaking of bread.

433. Did Christ Come Only for the Jews?

The words of the Lord Jesus Christ, "I come but to the house of Israel," must be read in connection with the entire tenth chapter of the gospel through Matthew. When Christ came into the world, He came with the gospel of the Kingdom for Israel. When Israel rejected this message, He turned to the Gentiles. Israel placed Him upon the Cross, and put Him to death, and during this dispensation, Israel is set aside and He is calling out His body, the Bride of the Lord Jesus Christ, the Church. After this Bride is raptured and taken up into heaven with Himself, the Lord will begin to deal again with the house of Israel, and will re-gather them into the land of Palestine, and set up the Kingdom which He has promised throughout all the prophecies of the Old Testament.

434. If Christ Kept the Law Before Calvary, Was He Not Breaking the Law by Plucking Ears of Corn on the Sabbath Day As Recorded in Matthew 12:1?

> At that time Jesus went on the sabbath day through the corn; and his disciples were an hungred, and began to pluck the ears of corn, and to eat (Matt. 12:1).

You are making the same mistake that the Adventists and a great many others make in not distinguishing between the Law, and the traditions of the Law. When Christ "violated the sabbath," as you say, by picking corn, He was violating the "tradition" of the Pharisees and the Scribes. Jesus

Himself laid down the principle that it is good to do good
on the Sabbath Day. If you will remember that it was
"tradition," that Jesus violated, and not the "Law of God,"
I think you will have the solution to your problem.

435. According to the Calendar, What Year Are We in Now?

Concerning the Christian calendar, we do not know
exactly what year this is. We are positive that there is at
least a four year discrepancy in our present calendar, but
how much more we do not know. The Lord has purposely
allowed the calendar to get mixed up, lest we should begin
to set dates for the coming of the Lord. The calendar has
been changed so many times that today no one knows just
exactly when the Christian era began, and therefore, how
far along we are at this time.

436. What Is the Significance of Pomegranates on the High Priest's Robe?

Concerning the pomegranate, it was a fruit which grew
in Palestine, and was a symbol of great fruitfulness. It is
usually understood by Bible students that the red seeds
of the pomegranate speak of the atoning blood, and the
seeds which are so numerous speak of fruitfulness. For
this reason the priest carried figures of pomegranates on
the border of his garments as he went in to minister in the
sanctuary. We believe that all these things have a spiritual
significance and when we get to glory we shall understand
them completely.

437. Why Did People Live So Much Longer in the Years before the Flood?

In regard to the longevity of the antediluvians, those who
lived before the flood, there are two reasons for this. The
first, there was as yet no written revelation of God, and
the knowledge of the Lord was maintained by oral tradition
from father to son. There were as a result only a few gen-

erations between Adam and Moses, who wrote the first
books of the Bible. The Lord, therefore, permitted people
to live that long so the knowledge of the Lord would not be
lost.

Second, the human race had not yet degenerated through
generations and generations of sinning.

438. What Is the Meaning of the Number "40" in Scripture?

It is a well-known fact that the numerals in Scripture
all have a real spiritual significance. Every number in the
Bible where it is repeated has a significance which is constant throughout the Scripture. Most Bible students believe
that the number, "40," is the number of preparation.
Throughout the Bible we find that 40 days are usually con-
sumed in preparing for some great event, such as the giving
of the law, and the warning of Jonah, etc. It speaks of the
period of time which God usually gives to the nations or
peoples in warning them before the real judgment falls
upon them.

439. How Do We Know If We Are Led of the Spirit?

It is well to remember, in seeking the will of the Lord,
that the Lord never leads us to do anything which is not in
perfect harmony with His revealed will, as given in the
Word of God. When there is any doubt in our minds, it
is always better to wait until we have some definite token
from the Word of God which makes us sure that we are
traveling in the direction in which He is leading. Sometimes the Lord does not immediately show us the way
in order that our faith may be tested, and thereby also
strengthened.

I do not know any better way of knowing the leading
of the Holy Spirit than to become more and better ac-
quainted with the Word of God. The more we know of His

Word, the more we know of His will, and the easier it will be to discern just where He leads us.

440. What Is the Significance of "Whirlwind" in the Bible?

Concerning the significance of whirlwinds, as used in Job, Ezekiel and Nahum, and various other passages, the opinion among Bible expositors seems to be that the whirlwind speaks of one of the manifestations of God's judgment. It is usually associated with God's intervention in behalf of His people, and in sending judgment upon the enemies of the saints.

In order to understand Job 38, we need to go back to Job 37:9, where one of the friends of Job mentions the whirlwind in connection with the manifestation of the power of God. I believe that the best translation of Job 38:1 is as follows: "Then the Lord answered *for* Job out of the whirlwind, and said, Who is this that darkeneth counsel by words without knowledge?" Of course, these words are not addressed to Job, but they are addressed to Elihu who gave his wonderful speech in the preceding chapter, Job 37. If we accept this position that God is not answering Job here, but rather answering Job's accusers, then of course, the interpretation becomes more simple. This is also in harmony with the other passages which you mentioned. The whirlwind indicates God's vindication of His own in the judgment that He sends upon their enemy.

441. In Studying and Reading the Book of Joshua, I Am Wondering Why God Permitted So Many Innocent People To Be Killed?

It is not easy to understand why God commanded Israel to destroy the nations, until we read the first and second chapters of Romans, and we find there that sin had so corrupted human nature, that God must send His judgment upon them. After all, God destroyed the nations before the flood, also, and spared only Noah. We must remember that God is loving and kind, but is also holy and righteous, and just and true, and will not spare the wicked but will punish sin, no matter where and when it is committed. I trust this will help you to understand this problem a little bit better. When we get to heaven we shall know all about it, and there will be no more doubt in our minds. If God permitted wicked men to continue unrestrained, the knowledge of God would soon vanish from the earth.

442. Is Capital Punishment Scriptural?

There is a great diversity of opinion among Bible students on this matter. It seems to have been instituted way back in the beginning after the flood when God says, "Whoso sheddeth man's blood, by man shall his blood be shed" (Genesis 9:6). Many base their belief in capital punishment upon this particular passage. I also realize that there are many others who do not accept this explanation, and who are strongly opposed to all forms of capital punishment.

It seems to me it is a matter of individual and personal conviction, and every man should be persuaded in his own mind. I certainly would not judge people for believing one way or another. I believe that there are sincere Christians on both sides of some of these questions, which it would be impossible for us to settle until we meet the Lord face to face. My personal opinion is that capital punishment for deliberate murder is entirely Scriptural.

443. When Christ Said to Peter, "Before the Cock Crow" Did He Mean a Certain Time of the Day or Was It the Literal Crowing of a Cock?

The "cock crow" was an expression used in ancient time for the announcement of the morning watch. The morning watching, just before the break of day, was called the "cock crow," and so it is possible that it may refer to the morning watch.

The fact that a cock did crow makes me think that it was an actual, literal cock that did crow at the time that Peter denied his Lord. The fact that the gospels state that "before the cock crows," and "the cock crows twice," offers no obstacle since the Lord does not say before the cock crow *once*, but "before the cock crows," and in Mark says "before the cock crows twice." The one, therefore, supplements the other.

444. I Would Like to Have an Explanation Concerning the Ten Virgins.

There is a wide difference of opinion among Bible teachers and scholars. There are some who believe that all of this belongs to the tribulation period and refers to the nation of Israel. The five wise virgins, therefore, would be the faithful Jews who will be saved during the tribulation period, and described as the 144,000 in Revelation 7 and 14. The foolish virgins, according to this interpretation, are the unsaved Israelites who will perish in the tribulation.

Then there is the other interpretation which applies to the Church, and teaches that the five wise virgins are those who have been truly born again, and are saved, and will enter the Kingdom, while the foolish virgins are those who have not been saved, who merely have a profession of salvation, but have never received Christ as their personal Saviour, and, therefore, will be lost.

Then there is a third interpretation, generally held by the Pentecostal churches, that the wise virgins are those who have received the second blessing, and are leading the victorious life, and will, therefore, be raptured before the tribulation, while the foolish virgins are those who are saved but lead a defeated life and have not received the second definite work of grace, and therefore, will pass through the tribulation period.

Personally, I believe that the primary interpretation is to the nation of Israel, and by application it is also true of Christians, that those who are truly saved are represented by the wise virgins, and those who have never experienced the new birth but merely make a profession are represented by the foolish virgins.

445. Why Were the Pigeon and Turtledove Not Divided in the Old Testament Sacrifice the Way the Larger Animals Were? (Genesis 15)

In regard to your question, concerning the pigeon and the turtledove, it was the law in the Old Testament that while the larger animals had to be divided as signifying the broken body and the shed blood of the Lord Jesus Christ, the pigeon and the turtledove had to do with cleansing and sanctification rather than with justification. Since the ox and the heifer, the goat and lamb all pointed to the work of Christ upon the Cross, they had to be divided, but since the pigeon and the turtledove look especially toward the resurrection of the Lord Jesus Christ in a typical sense, they were not divided.

446. What Is the Significance of the Phrase, "See Thou Tell No Man," Found in the Passages in Matthew 8:4, Mark 8:26 and 30, and Mark 9:30?

The reason the Lord Jesus told His disciples not to publish the message was that this was the message to Israel which was the "mystery" only to be revealed after the rejection and the Cross. Romans 11:25 plainly tells us that blindness must come upon Israel, until the fulness of the Gentiles comes in. Healing belongs to the kingdom age, and Jesus, anticipating His rejection, told them not to publish this message.

447. If the Days of Creation Were Days of Twenty-four Hours Each, and the World Is About Six Thousand Years Old, How Do the Scientific Findings of Pre-Historic Dinosaurs, etc., Fit into the Bible Record of Creation?

In regard to what you had to say concerning the six days, I am quite in agreement about the record in Genesis of the creation of light, vegetation, animals and man as given in the first few chapters, that the days spoken of were literal days of twenty-four hours each. However, the original creation of the earth, calling it out of nothing, as recorded in Genesis 1:1 is quite a different matter, and may date back to an indefinite period of time. The original creation as found in Genesis 1:1 may have taken eons or ages. The seven days of twenty-four hours each refer to the re-creation beginning in verse 2. There is an indefinite period of time between Genesis 1:1 and Genesis 1:2.

448. If God Deals with Man in Days of 1,000 Years Each and We Are About to the End of the First Six Thousand Years, Would It Not Be Possible to Set an Approximate Date for the Lord's Return?

God deals in a week of seven days of one thousand years each, according to Psalm 91, and II Peter 3. The six days of man's labor and failure are almost at an end, and we believe that we are on the very threshold of the millennial day of God's reign upon the earth through Jesus Christ. It certainly seems as though it is time for the Lord to come. Of course, we do not know exactly how far along we are, since the calendar has been confused. The Lord has deliberately not allowed us to know the exact chronology since man was created, lest we should be given to setting days and hours of the Lord's return. We know that there is a discrepancy of at least four years, and how many more before that we do not know. All we do know is that it seems to be near. The Lord Jesus said, "When these things begin to come to pass, then look up, and lift up your heads; for your redemption draweth nigh" (Luke 21:28).

449. I Have Had Some Unusual Dreams, and Am Wondering If You Could Be of Some Help to Me in Understanding Them.

I do not believe that dreams and visions and revelations are for this dispensation at all. The only revelation which God gives us in this age is found within the pages of the Bible, and we can give no attention to dreams and other manifestations such as you record. My advice to you would be to forget all about your dreams, and occupy yourself with a study of the Word of God in which we have all that the Lord wishes to reveal to us. We have a great many people who write in to us concerning visions and dreams which they too have had, but it is our firm conviction that they are of no significance whatsoever.

450. How Could There Be Day and Night Without the Sun and Moon? The Bible Speaks of "Evening and Morning" Three Days Before the Sun Was Placed on the Fourth Day.

We must remember that the sun and moon were created on the fourth day to be lightbearers. The light was there before in a diffused way, but not in the sense that it was contained within these bodies and reflected on the moon. We know, today, for instance, that there is light independent of the sun and the moon and the stars. It is sometimes called radio-light and sometimes cosmic light. It is not necessary for the sun and the moon to be present in order that there may be light and darkness.

451. Did the Israelites Build the Pyramids Under Pharaoh in Exodus?

There is no record whatsoever that the Israelites built the pyramids. This is merely a supposition that some people have made, but there is no evidence of it in the Scripture or elsewhere.

452. Would You Please Recommend a Good Commentary for Bible Study?

It is rather difficult to suggest one single volume. However, "Matthew Henry" has been standard for many, many years, and while it is sound in the fundamental doctrines, it is not pre-millennial, and does not give much light on the truth of the second coming. However, it is a valuable book. May I suggest that you get individual books from fundamental Bible teachers. All of the books by Dr. Arno C. Gabelein, Dr. William L. Pettingill, Dr. H. A. Ironside, and Dr. Lewis Sperry Chafer are very good. I would suggest that you try and get their books on the various parts of the Bible.

453. To What Do Fig Leaves Refer in Scripture?

If you will just remember that fig leaves in Scripture always refer to profession, without life or possession, you will see the application to the nation of Israel. The first mention of fig leaves is in Genesis, and there represents man's effort to cover his nakedness of sin by the work of his own hands instead of the gift of God as seen in the animal skins in Genesis 3:21. Fig leaves represent self-righteousness. It was the peculiar sin of Israel. (See Matthew 21:19; Mark 11:13, and Romans 10:3)

CHAPTER 18

PRAYER

454. Where Does the Lord's Prayer Fit In, Dispensationally?

"The Lord's Prayer" is found in the Sermon on the Mount, which is the constitution of the Kingdom Age. The Lord's Prayer is on the ground of the law and not of grace. For instance, in this dispensation we do not want to be forgiven as we forgive those who trespass against us, but rather, we forgive one another because we have already been forgiven. This prayer will fit into the Kingdom age, and particularly into the tribulation.

455. What Is Your Opinion Concerning Repeating the Lord's Prayer with Our Family before Meals?

I do not see any harm in using the Lord's prayer, although when it is just used as a form, and a part of an order of worship, I see no value in it. The Lord's Prayer, of course, is a kingdom prayer by interpretation, and the sad part is that it is used by many Christians as a sort of charm.

456. I Have Prayed for Years for the Salvation of My Loved Ones and Have Not Yet Seen My Prayers Answered. Do You Think I Should Continue to Pray for Them? They Seem Farther Away from the Lord Now Than They Have Ever Been.

In regard to your problem, there is a great deal of promise in the Bible that if we will pray for our loved ones, they will be saved. Scripture tells us definitely that it is not God's will that any should perish, but that all should come to repentance, and if we pray in the will of

God, the Lord Jesus Christ said He would hear us, so when we pray for the salvation of our loved ones we are praying in His will, and we have a right to claim the promise. He may not always answer us at the time that we expect, and it may not always be in the way that we look for it, but if we will firmly continue to trust and not for one moment doubt the Lord, we have a right to believe that our prayers will be honored and will be answered.

457. Is There a Special Pattern of Prayer to Follow?

I believe the Lord teaches each one of us to pray in our own acceptable way unto Him, but in the Lord's Prayer we do have a pattern. It is brief, to the point, without needless repetition and covers all our needs. We should ask the Lord Himself to "teach us to pray."

458. My Husband Passed Away Some Time Ago. Is It All Right for Me to Continue to Pray for Him?

In regard to your question concerning prayer for your husband, since he is at home and with the Lord, there is no occasion or need for your prayers anymore. He is under the direct and personal supervision and presence of the Lord Jesus Christ. Just look forward to that day when you will meet him again. That is the blessed Hope which we as believers have in Christ Jesus.

459. Why Should We "Pray for the Peace of Jerusalem" As We Find It in Psalm 122:6?

Concerning praying for the peace of Jerusalem, you must remember that this is a prophetic prayer. Peace will not come until in God's program Israel is back in the land, so when we pray for the peace of Jerusalem, we are praying for the coming of their Messiah, the Lord Jesus Christ and the setting up of the Kingdom. Only then will peace come. It is the same as praying, "Thy Kingdom come, Thy will be done in earth, as it is in heaven."

460. Does God Answer the Prayers of Children?

The Lord does not hear the prayers of sinners, we know, but I do not believe that I would want to go on record as saying that God does not hear the prayers of little children. They are not yet conscious sinners, and I do believe that the Lord Jesus does hear their prayer. I cherish above all things the fact that my mother taught me to pray when I was just a little lad, and later on these prayers came back to me, and certainly were a means for my conversion in later life. We should urge our children as soon as they are old enough to understand, to definitely receive the Lord as their personal Saviour.

461. Do You Think That We Should Pray for the Lord's Return When There Are Still So Many Who Need to Be Saved?

In regard to praying for the Lord's immediate return in the light of the fact that there are still many who are not saved, you must remember that every moment which the Lord tarries there are thousands of people born in this world who will ultimately be lost, so that the sooner the Lord comes, the less there will be who will be lost in the end.

462. I Have Been Taught That We Should Pray with our Face Toward Jerusalem, and Continue to Do This. I Would Like to Have Your Opinion on This Practice.

You must realize, when we pray, we pray unto God, the Father, in the name of the Lord Jesus Christ who is in heaven. However, I do not believe it makes any difference which way our face happens to be turned. I do not want to judge you, and if you feel that you receive a spiritual inspiration from assuming your attitude toward Jerusalem, I see no reason why you should not continue that way. Just do what the Lord leads you to do, and pay no attention to what others may think. After all, "Unto his own master

every man standeth or falleth" (Romans 14:4). The
practice of facing Jerusalem was for the Jews, not for us.

463. I Would Like Some Help on the Expression in the Lord's Prayer, "Lead Us Not Into Temptation."

In regard to the prayer, "Lead us not into temptation,"
this is a Kingdom prayer, and must be taken in the light
in which the Lord Jesus Christ gave it to us. The purpose
of it seems to be to ask the Lord for strength in the
hour of trial and temptation in order that we may gain the
victory. It ought to be our constant prayer, that the Lord
may give us the strength that we need, that when temptations come we may find His help at all times sufficient.

464. Why Should We Pray for Those in Authority in Our Land, If God's Plan for the Ages Must Be Worked Out Anyway?

It is not easy to answer questions such as this, but the
Bible distinctly tells us that we must pray for those who
are in authority (I Timothy 2:1-2). It is perfectly true
that God has a plan and if we pray contrary to this plan,
the Lord will not hear us. We know that the prophecies of
the Word of God cannot be broken, and therefore, we
should seek always to pray in the will of God, and according to the revealed will of God as given in the Scriptures.

I believe that there is much useless praying because we
are praying for things which God already has predicted
would not come to pass. I do not believe that we have a
right to pray for permanent peace on earth until after the
Lord Jesus Christ returns. However, since we do not
know when He is coming, I believe that it is perfectly
legitimate to pray for a period of peace at least if the Lord
should tarry, during which we may continue to send out the
blessed Gospel of the Lord Jesus Christ. We have to seek
and search the Scriptures, that we may be able to pray
intelligently concerning these matters.

CHAPTER 19

PROPHECY

465. When Will the Mark of the Beast Be Given?

The mark of the beast will be given after the church is gone. Those who receive the mark of the beast cannot be saved. It will be a mark given to individuals signifying their allegiance to the antichrist. Just what the mark will be we do not know. The same is true of the beast. The beast will not be revealed until after the rapture of the Church (II Thessalonians 2).

466. Is There Any Record in Scripture Regarding the Place of the United States in Prophecy?

While many things are clear in prophecy, there is a wide difference of opinion in regard to the place of the United States in the final set-up. It is best not to go beyond that which is written, but trust the Lord and eagerly wait for the coming of His Son. We do know that the United States will be among the "all nations" described in the final battle of the world in Joel 3:1.

467. What Is the Significance and Meaning of the Number of the Beast — 666?

The nearest that we can come to the meaning of the number of the beast, 666, is that six is the number of man, and three is the number of completeness. Thus three sixes would indicate the number of a super-man, which no doubt the antichrist will be.

468. Why Is the Tribe of Dan Left Out of the 144,000?

According to Jacob's prophecy in the forty-ninth chapter of Genesis, verse 17, it is evident that the antichrist, the Man of Sin, will come out of the tribe of Dan, of whom Judas was a type. For this reason, Dan is left out and another substituted.

Ephraim is not mentioned, and Joseph substituted because Ephraim became the name for the northern ten tribes.

469. Will Carnal Christians Go Through the Tribulation?

At the rapture, according to I Thessalonians 4, all who sleep in Christ will be caught away. Jesus used not only the expression, "as it was before the flood, so shall it be in the day of the coming of the Son of man," but He also said, "as it was in the days of Sodom and Gomorrah." Not only was Noah saved before the judgment of the flood which is a type of the tribulation, but carnal Lot was also delivered before the destruction of Sodom, another type of the tribulation, according to Jesus. However, the carnal Christian will suffer loss at the judgment seat of Christ (I Corinthians 3:11-15).

470. If Christ Comes As a Thief in the Night, Then How Can "Every Eye See Him?"

You confuse the *rapture* of the church *before* the tribulation, and the *second coming* of Christ *after* the tribulation. When He comes before the tribulation, He comes as a thief to take away the saved. When He comes after the tribulation, He comes to judge the wicked. This will be the public appearing when every eye shall see Him. The fact that the unbelievers will not hear the shout or the voice, can easily be explained when you realize that all people do not hear radio programs either, unless they are tuned in to the right wave length.

471. Will the Antichrist Be the Pope of Rome, and Where Does the Roman Catholic Church Fit into Bible Prophecy?

The antichrist will come out of the tribe of Dan and will be a Jew. The Roman Catholic church, together with all other apostate religions, is the scarlet woman of Revelation 17 and 18 and her illegitimate brood. The Pope will not be the antichrist.

472. What Is the "Mystery of Iniquity"?

The Mystery of Iniquity is Satan himself, who is now hiding his identity, but after the rapture of the Church will incarnate himself in a human being, called the antichrist, or the Man of sin. Today he is called the "mystery of iniquity who already worketh" (II Thess. 3).

473. Will the Roman Catholic Church Be the Religious Leader During the Tribulation?

Concerning Roman Catholicism, there is no question in my mind that after the rapture all the churches left behind without any born-again Christians in them, will unite in a great world-wide federation in which the Catholic church will undoubtedly be the leader (Revelation 17 and 18).

474. Will the Jews Be Back in Jerusalem before Christ Returns?

I do not believe that the Jews will return into the land of Palestine in full until after the rapture of the Church of Jesus Christ. They will be brought there by these two methods; first, by the desire for a homeland (as seen in the present movement of thousands of Jews into Palestine) and secondly, the full return will be in response to the false promises of the false christ, the antichrist, who will not appear until after the Church has been taken out.

475. Will There Be a Period of Prosperity Before or After the Rapture?

Concerning a period of prosperity before or after the rapture, I must confess that I am somewhat at a loss as to just what it is you are referring. I do not find anything in the entire Bible which speaks of a period of prosperity before the Lord has to come. However, there is a hint of a limited period of prosperity immediately after the rapture when the antichrist will bring about a false millennium as represented by the white horse of Revelation 6. I do not believe, however, that there is any definite statement concerning such a period. The apostle Paul and the Lord Jesus Christ are very clear in telling us that in the last days perilous times shall come, as given so clearly in the twenty-fourth chapter of Matthew, and the first and second epistles of Timothy.

476. Someone Told Me That the 144,000 Jews Saved After the Rapture Will Be Killed During the Tribulation. Is This Right?

I am rather surprised that anyone should teach that the 144,000 would be killed. I believe that these are the remnant represented by the type, Noah, and will pass through the tribulation period, and be supernaturally preserved by the Lord. A careful reading of Revelation, chapters 7 and 14, I think will verify this position. I believe that the difficulty arises from the fact that during the tribulation, great multitudes of believers from among the Gentiles will lay down their lives and have part in that last resurrection at the end of the tribulation period which will complete the body of Christ (see particularly Revelation 20). These are the company that complete the first resurrection.

I certainly do not believe that the 144,000 Jews will be killed, but that they will go into the millennial kingdom to be God's great representatives of the truth.

477. What Will Happen to the Children When the Church of Christ Is Raptured?

Since we believe that all the saved will be raptured, and none be left behind, it follows that all children before the age of accountability will necessarily also be caught away. We believe that people are only lost because of rejection of the Lord Jesus Christ, and since children cannot reject the Lord, all of them are saved. There is nothing in the Bible to substantiate infant damnation; therefore, we believe that all children will be raptured.

478. When Will the Atomic Bomb Be Used?

I believe that there will be atomic destruction during the tribulation period. However, the final destruction as foretold by Peter in II Peter will not come until after the millennium.

479. If Russia's Invasion of Palestine Takes Place about the Middle of the Tribulation, What About Ezekiel 39:9-10? Will They Be Burning Those Weapons in the Millennium?

In regard to your question concerning Russia's invasion of Palestine, there may be some apparent difficulty about the fact that it will take seven years to clean up the debris which will be left after the battle in Ezekiel 39. However, this should cause no difficulty whatsoever, since the Battle of Armageddon will take place about three and one-half years after the battle with Russia, and so there may be a double accumulation of destructive war materials which will fit into the entire picture. We must remember that the Battle of Armageddon comes at the end of the tribulation, while Russia's invasion is in the middle of the tribulation. There is no question that there will be remembrance and memory of the awful tribulation in the millennium, otherwise how could they be thankful for the deliverance which God has given them.

480. When Will the Out-Pouring of the Holy Spirit and the Redemption of Creation Take Place?

Concerning the second out-pouring of the Holy Spirit and the redemption of creation, you must remember that during the tribulation period, after the first half has already passed, the spirit of the Lord will be poured out upon Israel, and they will be converted, and become the 144,000 missionaries of Revelation 7, and as a result a great number of Gentiles will be saved, as also recorded in this same chapter.

This same outpouring of the Spirit will also affect all creation, so that as a result of it, in the millennium after Jesus comes the second time, the animal and vegetable creation will also be redeemed according to Paul's words in Romans, chapter 8. This is in accordance with many prophecies including Isaiah 11 and 35. The results need not be immediate, but it will come when the curse is removed at the second coming of the Lord Jesus Christ.

The great tribulation is a brief period of intense agony upon the earth, lasting about three and one-half years. Just at what stage during the tribulation the Spirit will be poured out, is not indicated, but it will result in the blessings described at the close of that period.

481. How Do We Conclude That the Tribulation Will Last for Seven Years?

In regard to the seven years' tribulation period, there are two lines of Scripture which indicate this length of time. The first is that one week of Daniel's seventy weeks is still unfulfilled, and since these are weeks of years, we know that the tribulation will last seven years.

Then, too, the last half of the tribulation, called the "great tribulation," will be exactly three and one-half years, 1260 days, or forty-two months, according to the book of Revelation. Since this will begin with the setting up of the image of the beast in the middle of the tribulation, the entire tribulation must be seven years.

Chapter 20

SALVATION

482. Does the Bible Teach "Eternal Security?"

While the term, "eternal security," does not occur anywhere in the Scriptures, we do believe that God does impart eternal life to all who believe on Him (John 10:28-29 and I John 5:13).

You must remember that while the expression, "eternal security," is not found in the Bible, the Word of God does definitely teach eternal life, and our Lord says in John 10:28, "they shall never perish." This verse certainly seems to teach that the Lord is faithful, and therefore, when we put our trust in Him, we can say with Paul, "I know whom I have believed, and am persuaded that he is able to keep that which I have committed unto him against that day" (II Timothy 1:12).

There are many believers who violently reject the doctrine of security, but if they are truly saved, they are just as secure, even though they do not believe in this security. They miss the joy and peace, but not the security.

483. I Think That I Am Saved, But How Can I Be Sure?

If you will read the first epistle of John, and underscore the word, "know," every time it occurs, it will help you greatly. Remember, your salvation depends upon the finished work of Christ and not upon your own righteousness or experience or feelings. It is entirely a matter of believing that Christ did it all. It is not our faith, but His faithfulness which saves us.

484. I Know That I Am Saved, but Am Not Able to Give the Day and Hour Like Many Whom I Hear Testify. Is This Necessary for Salvation?

There are many of God's dear children who have been brought up in a different atmosphere who may not know the exact moment when they were saved. The important thing is to know it *now*. I will agree that it is desirable to be able to point back to a certain moment, but I do not believe it to be essential. Everyone has not been brought up in the same environment as you and I have.

485. Should We Pray for the Unsaved? If God Has Predestined Them to Be Lost, How Can Our Prayers Be Answered?

I believe the Scriptural doctrine of predestination, based on the foreknowledge of God. Since God is omniscient, He knew everything beforehand, and could plan accordingly. This does not eliminate the value of prayer, since predestination is God's business, and believing is ours. If we will do our part faithfully, we need have no worry about God fulfilling His part.

486. Will the Unsaved Have Another Chance for Salvation after the Rapture of the Church? If so, How, Since the Holy Spirit Will Be Gone?

We do believe that there will be great multitudes saved in the tribulation according to Revelation chapter 7, but those who deliberately and wilfully refuse the Lord *now*, certainly cannot expect a second chance after the Lord comes. I have always held that those who wilfully reject the Gospel will not be given another opportunity.

After the Holy Spirit is taken away in the rapture, He will still be present in the world, just as He was before He came on the day of Pentecost, as the omnipresent person of the Godhead. In His abiding presence with the Church,

He will be raptured with the Church, but in His omni-
presence as God will continue to be on the earth.

487. How Can I Know That I Am Really Born Again?

In answering your question, may I suggest to you that
you must put no faith whatsoever in feelings, or in the
opinions of men or even in the logic of your own heart.
Everything depends upon the promise of the Lord. Faith is
the victory. When we look at our own hearts and our own
lives, there is much cause to doubt. However, when we look
at the promises of God, there can be no doubt. After all,
the Bible says, "Whosoever shall call upon the Name of the
Lord shall be saved." You will notice that there are no
strings tied to that promise. If you have sincerely called
upon His Name, then God says you are saved, whether you
always feel it or realize it or not. And may I repeat again,
your salvation does not depend upon what you think, but
upon what you believe; not upon what you feel, but upon
what God says, and He says, "Him that cometh unto Me, I
will in no wise cast out."

488. Does the Bible Teach "Household Salvation?"

Concerning household salvation, you must remember that
in the household of the Philippian jailor, in Acts 16:31,
all the members believed. If the house is to be saved, all
must believe. Moreover, if we are saved and fully trust the
Lord for the salvation of our children, He will keep His
Word, "Train up a child in the way he should go: and
when he is old, he will not depart from it" (Proverbs
22:6).

489. I Know That I Have Been Saved, But Many Times I Doubt My Salvation and Don't Feel Saved. Does This Mean That I Have Never Really Been Born Again?

I can quite easily understand your emotions as expressed
in your letter, for although it may surprise you, I too doubt

many times. I do not doubt my Saviour or the Word of
God, but I often doubt a certain fellow by the name of
De Haan. When I look within, all is dark, but when
I look to Him and His promises, all is bright. This pre-
scription ought to work for you too. I wonder whether
you are not looking at yourself instead of your Saviour.
Remember, your feelings change, but God's promises are
always the same.

490. Are All People Born the Children of God?

In regard to your question whether everyone is a
child of God, the Bible definitely states that by birth, we
are *not* the children of God, but children of wrath, and
children of the devil. Only by the new birth, through
faith in Jesus Christ, can one become a servant and child
of God.

491. Is It Ever Too Late in This Life to Come to God?

I do not believe that it is ever too late to repent and to
come to the Lord Jesus Christ. If it were possible for one
to get to a point that he cannot repent or come to the
Lord anymore, he or she would be totally unconscious of
it. They would be completely, spiritually dead. Therefore,
for that reason, I believe that everyone who is even concerned about the question is still in a position to come to
the Lord Jesus Christ. The Bible is clear that "whosoever
shall call upon the name of the Lord shall be saved"
(Romans 10:13), and again, "if we confess our sins, He
is faithful and just to forgive us our sins, and to cleanse
us from all unrighteousness" (I John 1:9). There are no
conditions attached to these promises, but they are for
"whosoever," and for everyone and include every Adam's
son and daughter who may come to Christ in confession.
We must, of course, believe His Word, and that His Word
is true.

492. Someone Told Me That According to Deuteronomy 23:2, an Illegitimate Child Could Not Be Saved. Is This Taught in the Bible?

There is nothing in the Bible whatsoever to indicate that a child born out of wedlock cannot be saved just as well as anyone else. "Whosoever will" may receive the Lord Jesus Christ by faith, and certainly something over which the child has no control cannot affect him in the least.

CHAPTER 21

WOMEN

493. Do You Think That Christian Women Should Adorn Themselves According to the Fashions Set by the World?

The Bible is clear that Christians are not to follow the form and fashions and fads of the world, but on the other hand, our bodies are the temple of the Holy Ghost, and we have a right to dress them properly. If one is naturally pale, I do not see that a slight amount of color would be wicked in itself, although I personally abhor the use of fingernail polish, lipstick, the plucking of the eyebrows and an excess of rouge. These things are of the world, and have no place in the Christian's conduct.

494. Did God Sanction Polygamy in the Old Testament? Abraham, David and Solomon Had More Than One Wife and It Does Seem That God Sanctioned This Practice.

God permitted those things, but there is not a single verse in Scripture where God either endorsed or encouraged or blessed it. His original creation was one man and one woman, and the sad results of every case of polygamy as related in the Scriptures is God's own commentary on the evils of polygamy. Read carefully I Kings 11.

495. What Is the Significance of Long Hair, and Why Is the Woman Forbidden to Have Her Hair Cut?

The figure of the marriage relationship is a figure of the relationship of Christ to His Church as His Bride (Ephesians 5). In order to honor the subjection of the Church

to her head, the Lord Jesus Christ, the woman is to be
subject to her own husband, and since hair is the glory
of the woman (I Corinthians 11:15), long hair becomes a
testimony of her submission to the Lord Jesus Christ.

496. Must a Woman Wear a Hat in Church?

I am of the firm conviction that the passage in I Corinthians 11 dealing with keeping the head covered has to
do with the glory of woman, which is her hair and not her
hat. The Bible teaches that a woman should keep her head
covered with hair. Moreover, the passage in Corinthians
speaks of conduct at the Lord's table, and that too should
be taken into consideration.

497. What Is the Place of the Woman in the Church?

When the assembly is gathered together in a Scriptural
way, then a woman's place is one of silence so far as
ministry is concerned. Three things are forbidden to
women. First, they must not interrupt meetings where the
Holy Spirit is at work, by asking questions (I Cor.
14:23-35).

Secondly, a woman must not set herself up as an authority in matters of doctrine, like an apostle (I Tim. 2:12).

Thirdly, a woman must not be put in a place of authority in the church. The place of authority is given to
the man. This is no slight upon the woman. It is simply
the recognition of her proper place in nature. It is not
a matter of superiority or of inferiority, but it is a matter
of order.

Regarding a woman teaching a Sunday school class, this
has nothing to do with the prohibitions mentioned above,
since such a class does not constitute an assembly of God.

498. Are Women Permitted to Do Any Speaking in the Church?

Concerning women speaking in the church, I fear that there has been a great deal of unnecessary misunderstanding. We must remember that the injunction of Paul that the women should keep silence in the church is connected with the admonition not to usurp authority over the man. I believe what God means is simply this, that a woman is not to take the authority over the man in the church, not to rule over him, for as you know, the man is the head of the woman, as Christ is the Head of the Church. I do not believe that it is wrong for a woman who has been blessed of the Lord with the gift of teaching to use her talents in the assembly for teaching other women. She is permitted to pray publicly, to testify and to instruct, but please notice again, that it must always be under the direction and in obedience to the man.

499. Does the Bible Forbid the Wearing of Wedding Rings and Other Jewelry?

I do not see that there is anything in the Bible which forbids the wearing of rings. The father placed a ring upon the hand of his wayward son when he returned. I believe that the Bible teaches that we should not go to extremes and excesses in adorning these bodies of ours, but feel that we should not go too far the other way either, in making the passage in I Peter 3:3 refer to the wearing of all jewelry. Peter warns against the "wearing of gold," and in the same connection also warns against the "wearing of apparel." It certainly does not mean that people should not wear clothes, but rather, that they should not set their heart upon these things and go to extremes.

500. Should a Christian Woman Obey Her Unbelieving Husband?

The question which you pose in your letter is one which can hardly be answered by a general statement. Each individual case demands individual attention. Of course, there should be no mixed marriages, for God strictly forbids Christians marrying unbelievers, but since many of them do, I believe that it is the will of the Lord according to I Corinthians 7 that the Christian should as far as possible live with her unbelieving husband and be obedient to him as far as she can, according to the Word of God, in an effort to influence him, and finally get him to receive the Lord Jesus. Of course, we must remember that obedience to God comes before everything, even before our obedience to government, husband and wife. "We should obey God rather than man." However, where a woman's obedience to her husband does not interfere with the plain teaching of the Word of God, I do believe that she should let her Christian testimony shine by even being the least, and obeying her husband in an effort to win him for the Lord Jesus.

501. As a Christian Mother, I Am Faced with the Problem of How to Dress My Little Children. If I Make Their Clothes Too Long, They Feel Out of Place with the Other Children, and Still I do Not Want to Follow the Pattern of the World for Them. Can You Help Me?

Concerning abbreviated apparel for children, I have long ago felt that modern fashions have gone to an unscriptural and dangerous extreme in permitting little children to go half or almost completely naked. They are brought up to be accustomed to nakedness, and when they grow older they continue. As a result, the older children, and even older people are wearing less and less clothes.

While I believe that our bodies should be comfortably dressed according to the temperature, I see no reason for exposing as much of the human body as is the custom today.

502. My Hair Is Very Thick, and Would Be Much Easier to Take Care of If I Had It Thinned by a Barber. I have Hesitated Having It Done Because I Know What the Bible Says about the Bobbing of Hair. What Do You Think I Should Do?

In regard to your question, I suppose that I am considered a crank when it comes to the matter of women's hair. I have always believed that Christian women should not have their hair bobbed, but of course, I also recognize that there are certain conditions when these things might be allowable. However, God has not appointed me to judge other people's conduct. I believe it is a matter which you have to decide between yourself and the Lord, and which cannot be decided by anyone else. I certainly would be the last one to criticize anyone for any action which they took in good conscience.

503. I Am Employed in a Factory Where It Is Compulsory for the Women to Wear Slacks. There Has Been No Question in My Mind But That This Was All Right Until One of My Friends Talked with Me about It, and I Would Like to Know What You Think about This.

I have read your problem with interest, and I feel that you ought to follow your own conscience in regard to this matter. If there is any question in your mind whatsoever, you may be sure that it would be wrong for you. The Bible says, "Let every man be persuaded in his own mind."

As for my own personal opinion, I believe that it is absolutely wrong for a woman to wear men's clothes (Deut. 22:5). It only ministers to the breakdown of the tender femininity of womanhood, and is a bad influence, and many of the evils of today can be traced to the habits of women copying men, and especially in the wearing of men's clothes. I personally feel that I would not want any of my own daughters to be dressed in the garb of men.

There is a difference, however, *where* these clothes are worn. There may be circumstances where wearing certain garb is necessary, but it should never be in public.

CHAPTER 22

WORLDLY AMUSEMENTS

504. I Am a High School Girl, and All of My Friends Attend the School Dances, and Though I Am a Christian, I Cannot See Anything Wrong with it. Do You Think I Am Doing Wrong By Going?

The Lord has given us a general rule covering not only dancing, but every other form of entertainment. Paul says to the Church, "Whatsoever ye do, do all to the glory of God." If you feel that spending precious time that should be used in winning souls on the dance floor is all right, you will have to answer to the Lord. The Bible says that whatsoever is not of faith is sin. I trust this will answer your question, and be of help to you. The fact that you raise the question at all is an indication that there is a doubt in your own mind. It is always safe to refrain from "doubtful" things.

505. Do You Think That Christians Should Take Part in the Worldly Amusements?

According to the Word of God, "all things are lawful, but all things do not edify." "All things are lawful," says Paul, "but all things are not expedient." We have a responsibility toward other Christians as well as toward the world, and while a man may not have conscience concerning a certain action, it becomes sin if it causes our brother to stumble. If you will read carefully I Corinthians 8, I think you will find the answer. Paul says that to do things which injure the brethren is sin. While we have liberty, we do not have license. Of course, if by "worldly" you mean "sinful" amusements, the answer is, of course, *no*. Christians should refrain from all such.

506. Do You Think That Card Playing Is Wrong? We Are Not Playing for Money, but Only for Recreation.

Many times the things that we may not think are wrong would be a stumbling block to some weaker Christian. Paul gives us a good rule to follow in I Corinthians 8:13. In the minds of the great majority of Christians card playing is associated with gambling and the world. While it may never lead to that in your case, yet in I Thessalonians 5:22 we are told to "abstain from all appearance of evil." I am sure that if you pray about this matter, the Lord will show you just what to do about it.

507. Do You Think That Christians Should Attend or Play Games, Such As Baseball, Football, Basketball, Etc.?

Concerning Christians attending baseball, football, basketball, etc., I hardly know what to answer you. I do not see any particular harm in boys and men playing these games if done in Christian fellowship. I realize that often times the environment is such that a Christian should not be found there at all, but we cannot be legalistic, and of course, we cannot judge the liberty of others who may have different views than we have. I believe that there is a place for recreation and for pleasure in the life of a Christian, and each individual ought to be his own judge as to whether he can do it to the glory of God, and to the praise of His Maker. Paul tells us, "Let every man be persuaded in his own mind." Personally, I don't have any time for baseball, football, basketball, etc., being kept so busy in the work of the Gospel. However, there are other forms of recreation which also cost money and in themselves are harmless. I think the whole thing depends upon whether it detracts us from our service of the Lord, and whether the environment and the company we keep is such that we would like to meet Him when He comes. I trust that this rather indefinite answer will be of some help to you.

508. Do You Think That Christians Should Participate in Gambling Games, and What Do You Think about Bingo If It Is Played in the Church Basement?

Not only is gambling absolutely contrary to the Word of God, because it puts its faith in chance and in fate rather than in the providence of Almighty God, but even our civil authorities who do not go by the Bible, outlaw gambling and think it is evil. Every state in the Union has certain laws against gambling, and even though they are not always enforced, it is the general consensus even among civil authorities that gambling is an evil. It is seeking to profit by the loss of someone else which is equivalent to stealing. I do not see how anyone can find any argument, either in reason, logic, decency or in the Bible in regard to this practice.

Of course, when it comes to doing these things in the church, it is entirely out of place. The church is the place for worship, the study of the Word of God, for prayer, and for fellowship around the broken Body of the Lord Jesus Christ. It is a stinging commentary on the evil of gambling that we read in the gospels, that when Jesus hung upon the Cross, the soldiers cast lots for His garments, and gambled over the possessions of our precious Lord. Gambling in the church, and playing bingo and those things in the house of God is just the same as what the soldiers did when they sat around the Cross and cast lots and gambled for the possessions of the Lord Jesus. I am sure that anyone who is truly born again, and wishes to do the will of God, would not even consider the evil of gambling, either in or outside of the church.

SUBJECT INDEX

Chapter 10

CHURCHES: THEIR SUPPORT
AND PROGRAM

Chapter 11

DIFFICULT SCRIPTURE
PASSAGES

SCRIPTURE REFERENCE INDEX

HOW TO USE:

This Scripture Reference Index has been arranged to help you make effective use of the book. The books of the Bible are arranged chronologically at the left of the columns with the chapter or verse reference indicated. On the right the question numbers are listed. For instance if you are interested in Chapter 27 of the book of Genesis, look for Chapter 27 under Genesis and you will find that question #169 refers to that chapter in Genesis. Or if you are interested in Luke 15:7, simply find Luke in this handy index and you will discover that Chapter 15, verse 7, is discussed in question #374. The questions are arranged in the book in chronological order and are in boldface type to make it easy for you to find them on the page.